ENDOR

Proverbs 29:18 in the Passion Translation says *"When there is no clear prophetic vision, people quickly wander astray. But when you follow the revelation of the word, heaven's bliss fills your soul."* In *The Power of Prophetic Vision*, Joan Hunter, uses her knowledge of the Word and her gift of relatability to inspire us to hear the voice of God, answer His call and impact the world we live in. Joan truly has a way of taking complicated spiritual subjects and making them easy and practical for believers to implement into their lives through her transparency, vulnerability and faith-filled walk. This book will release you into a greater place of fulfilled destiny as you embrace the power of your own prophetic vision.

JANE HAMON
Co-Apostle of Vision Church@Christian International
Author of *Dreams and Visions, The Deborah Company
The Cyrus Decree, Discernment*

Is there a part we play in our heavenly destiny fully manifesting on earth? Joan Hunter says, "yes," and wants to be your life coach to fulfill all God has for you in His Book of Life!

SID ROTH
Host, *It's Supernatural!*

A prophetic vision of God's dream for each person's life is absolutely crucial for every believer! I am excited to be able to endorse my friend, Joan Hunter's book, *The Power of Prophetic Vision*, on this subject because it is so important and so often neglected. All the worldly wisdom available to you through men will always fall far short of God's plan for you, but He is able to show you a way where there is no way!

Be encouraged as you put the principles in this book into practice and you will discover God's best for your life.

JOSHUA MILLS

The Power of

PROPHETIC

VISION

DESTINY IMAGE BOOKS BY JOAN HUNTER

Healing Starts Now!
Expanded Edition: Complete Training Manual

The Power of

PROPHETIC
VISION

How to Turn Your
Dreams into Destiny

JOAN HUNTER

DESTINY IMAGE® PUBLISHERS, INC.

P.O. Box 310, Shippensburg, PA 17257-0310

"Promoting Inspired Lives."

This book and all other Destiny Image and Destiny Image Fiction books are available at Christian bookstores and distributors worldwide.

Cover design by Eileen Rockwell
Interior design by Terry Clifton

For more information on foreign distributors, call 717-532-3040.

Reach us on the Internet: www.destinyimage.com.

ISBN 13 TP: 978-0-7684-5026-2
ISBN 13 eBook: 978-0-7684-5027-9
ISBN 13 HC: 978-0-7684-5029-3
ISBN 13 LP: 978-0-7684-5028-6

For Worldwide Distribution, Printed in the U.S.A.

1 2 3 4 5 6 7 8 / 23 22 21 20 19

ACKNOWLEDGMENTS

I want to say a special thank you to Destiny Image for helping me get this book in print and into your hands.

Naida Johnson, RN, CWS, FCCWS, and friend of over 50 years, who has helped me proof and work through this book and many others. One of my main intercessors.

CONTENTS

FOREWORD

*W*hen Joan Hunter asked me to write the foreword to her latest book, *The Power of Prophetic Vision: How to Turn Your Dreams into Destiny,* I was so excited! I said yes even though I really don't have a lot of time right now to do this. I heard from the Lord to do it because there is something that needs to be released to you through this book.

I figured the best way to demonstrate the message of "prophetic vision" is to slow down and listen to the Lord in the midst of busyness. I am not sure where you are or what you are going through. Busyness is one thing many of us have in common but also we all have the same amount of time.

I remember a mentor of mine years ago when I was always showing up late and missing deadlines. He said, "We all have 24 hours in a day and we all have access to the Lord."

Wow, that struck me deeply and sent me on a journey to try to better myself at time management, which I did not do a great job at. It was not until I started moving in harmony with the Lord that I began to master time. I now get more done in a week than most people do in a month. It is because I found a way to fulfill the prophetic vision and destiny of my life.

Once you step into your greater purpose and you understand some powerful principles of the Bible, it is like you are not even working when you are. The greatest fulfillment in life is when you find the calling the Lord has for you. For years I suffered in the wrong career and jobs that were not suited for me. I worked in credit management and bill collecting.

What? Doug Addison was a bill collector who calls you on the phone when you are about to sit down and eat? I did it because I got stuck in a place where I believed a lie that I could not do anything else and make good money. I also knew I had a call to full-time ministry but I could not go to Bible college and back then we did not have ministry schools and the internet like we do now.

But with God all things are possible; you only have to believe and ask Him for a strategy.

After leaving my full-time corporate job in 1994, I tried to work for my church to get training but I nearly went

bankrupt. The Lord called me to start a computer network-
ing business in San Francisco instead, something that I
really did not understand at the time and really did not want
to do—but I trusted the Lord. I had no idea that I was on
course with a huge discovery for my life and ministry.

During the mid-1990s I was the owner of my own
company and I had a unique job of installing and training businesses with their computer networks. So I would
come in and sit in their cubicles and fix and get things set
up. While I did this I noticed the Holy Spirit was giving
me prophetic pictures and words of knowledge for them.
I was able to share what I felt in a non-religious language
because it was San Francisco where people are not open
to Christianity.

Wow, I had no idea that I was pioneering prophetic
evangelism! I was doing this years before it was even discov-
ered in churches. And I was making a lot of money doing
it. A few years later we sold that business and planted some
churches and I became one of the forerunners of prophetic
evangelism, using prophecy and dream interpretation to
influence people for Jesus.

Like David said, I can take down Goliath because I
killed lions and bears while watching my father's sheep. God
will not waste a thing in your life. He is guiding you right
now and, like me, you are about to have a breakthrough discovery about your destiny. We went on to start my current
ministry, InLight Connection, and I became a prophetic
life coach.

Your destiny is like a connect-the-dots drawing that might not make sense right now. But each dot is a job, internship, training conference, or season of your life, good or bad. God wants to use it all once you trust Him and ask for His greater purposes to be revealed to you.

Your destiny is a unique calling from God that no one can fulfill but you. It involves getting to know Him better, growing in godly character, and helping people along the way!

I believe that you are reading this book by the design and calling of God. There are no coincidences in the Lord. You are about to have an encounter with the God of destiny in this book. Joan does a great job of anchoring things deeply in the Word of God and in the power of the Holy Spirit. I love her down-to-earth style of communicating. You feel like you are having a conversation with her and with the Lord at the same time.

My prayer for you is that you will discover more about the Lord, yourself, and your calling as you read this book!

Blessings,
Doug Addison
Author of *Hearing God Every Day: Understanding the Supernatural Ways God Speaks to Us*
DougAddison.com

Doug Addison is the founder and president of InLight Connection. Doug is a prophetic speaker, author, and coach. He is best known for his *Daily Prophetic Words* and *Spirit Connection* webcast, podcast, and blog. He and his wife Linda live in Los Angeles, California where they are impacting the arts and entertainment and media industries.

INTRODUCTION

God is preparing you to fulfill His plans for your life. I am so glad you chose to pick up this book because I believe its contents will give you greater insight into understanding your future. This instruction will open your eyes to visions and dreams that may not have been completely revealed to you in the past. God has exciting doors waiting to open for the resurrection of those dreams and visions. Once experienced, they become your memories so you can then dream again for even more insight.

There is so much power in this revelation. God wants you to know and understand further prophetic insights into your life as well as in your family's lives. It is so exciting when God gives me a special word for my children. Then I get to prophesy over my children.

1. This book will help you develop who you are meant to be and God's call on your life. This knowledge will allow you to walk out this revelation in a greater way with fulfillment and increased clarity.

2. Your dreams and visions are so important to your future. Understanding what God is doing in your life will open up your mind and heart to help others do the same.

3. Receiving a word from a prophet of God is always exhilarating and encouraging. It is always amazing to believe that God chose to send a word directly from His heart through a special man of God, specifically to me. He sends those treasured words to you also.

4. Sensitivity to His voice is key to being a willing vessel He can use and trust. Rarely does His prophetic words get long and lengthy with great detail. Often the word will be a few words or sentences. Whether an exhortation or warning, they are always treasures. If your word has been recorded, transcribe it. If necessary, write down what you heard. Include the date, occasion, and name of the prophet. Someday you will want to read those words again. It will fit into and confirm your dream or vision.

5. Are you ready to step into a new dimension of God's world here on earth? I believe it is but

a glimpse, a very important preview of what His heavenly world is like. Working through His children, He will communicate and touch others who need to feel and know the power of His love, His peace and His healing. Be prepared to learn so you can, in turn, show Him to others.

6. You will find prayers within this manuscript. Reading them silently is fine; however, reading them out loud is always best. Seeing and hearing those words have a unique impact on your spirit and mind. Let's start now.

Father, thank You for always providing me with the best resources for my development and growth in Your precious world. Open my heart and mind to what You have for me within these pages. Speak to me as only You can. And I will always give You my praise and worship because You are my God. Thank You for Your most precious gift, Your Son, Jesus. In His name. Amen.

Chapter 1

COULDA SHOULDA

*T*hroughout this book I share exciting teachings and revelations that God has given to me over the past few years, helping me get to where I am today.

One day I was asked, "Would you like to venture out and do different things in the ministry?"

I thought about it then answered, "No, not really."

"Do you want to be on television?"

"No."

"How about holding a microphone and talking to an audience?"

"No."

"Would you like to be in front of people?"

"No."

Those were some of the questions I was asked about fifteen or sixteen years ago. And all my answers were a definite "No." Yet today, I am doing all of those things for God.

This chapter is about "Coulda Shoulda." Our coulda's and shoulda's are the sad parts of our lives when we realize that we coulda done this or shoulda done that. We need to toss all of those thoughts out the window so we can see what we can do—today—for God.

Have you had these thoughts go through your mind? *Do I have what it takes to follow my calling? Do I feel as if the call has been taken from my life?* Shake off those feelings. God's call on your life will always remain there. The important thing is, what will you do with it? You may sit on it, you may throw it away, you may ignore it, you may talk yourself out of it, people may talk you out of it—or overwhelming circumstances and opportunities may detour you right out of the will of God. You should be very careful about the decisions you make when considering your God-given destiny.

Opportunities will come and go—and what you do with each one is what makes the difference between a so-so life and a life full of God's amazing and abundant blessings. You must understand that it's so very important that you follow the voice of God and do what He's called you to do.

You intended to harm me, but God intended it all for good. He brought me to this

position so I could save the lives of many people
(Genesis 50:20).

"I'm a Genesis 50:20 kind of woman," I tell people frequently. Though the enemy meant my past for evil, I took it, turned it around and made a miracle out of it. I made the devil sorry he ever did or tried to do anything to me. Once you understand that verse from the Bible, you'll realize that God can use every situation you go through for His glory.

I've had many, many opportunities to overcome problems in my life. Not just the potholes and holes in the ground I've had to hurdle. At times, I've been pushed into deep, dark caves. But I couldn't let any of those challenges destroy me. Instead, I filled them up, sealed them off, and kept going. And you can too.

But you reply, "Well, God gave me cancer." God doesn't give anyone cancer.

"Well, God made this person do that to me." God doesn't make people do things. He gave each of us free will to make our own choices.

Understand that different situations will challenge us. These can be brought on by the flesh, through other people or circumstances, or simply from life in general. Stop blaming the enemy or God—we make our own decisions, which can improve our situation or sometimes make things worse.

Someone may ask, "Why do children die?" Or say, "God took the child at a very young age." But God doesn't just "take" our children. Life and death happen—and our reaction to these events is what makes the difference.

Life happens—what we do next makes miracles happen.

I want to highlight several people in the Bible who took chilling challenges and daunting circumstances head-on and turned the situations into glory for God and success for themselves.

DAVID

The first one I want to mention is David. The Bible says that David was a man after God's own heart (Acts 13:22). He was also one of the greatest kings ever known. That's what most people know about King David, which is good; but if you look at his past and what happened to him, you realize he had sin in his life from making unwise decisions and choices. He was hardly the picture of perfection.

For instance, King David usually went to battle with his men; however, one day he sent the men to war while he stayed home because he had his eye on a beautiful lady named Bathsheba. Watching her bathe from his rooftop filled him with lust. Even though he knew she was married, he enticed her into an affair with him. By the way, he was already married also.

As if committing adultery wasn't sinful enough, David arranged for her husband to be killed. When he found out that Bathsheba was pregnant, he knew the baby was his, because her husband had been away fighting in the war. So, being king, he told his commander of the army to send Bathsheba's husband, Uriah, to the front lines, where he was killed. (See Second Samuel 11.)

Remember, this is the same man recorded in the Bible as being *"a man after God's own heart."* If you continue reading Second Samuel, you see that David married Bathsheba. She gave birth to the baby, but the child died soon after birth. The Lord was very displeased and sent His prophet Nathan to speak to David about his actions. Nathan told David the story of a rich man taking a poor man's only sheep. When David realized the story was about him, he repented.

What happened then? God took the situation, turned it around and made a miracle out of it. David had a heart transformation. He sought the heart of God and took responsibility for his sin, which redirected him back to his calling, his God-given destiny.

David needed a heart transformation. What does that mean? David wanted the heart of God. He wanted to live out God's calling, God's plan for his life. Before David died, he didn't look back and say, "I coulda shoulda." He had the heart of God. With God's help, David fulfilled his destiny despite his mistakes of earlier years.

I want the heart of God. I want to be able to love unconditionally and do anything and everything that God has called me to do. Yes, I make mistakes and I have to fall at

His throne and ask for His forgiveness. But I learn from my mistakes, get back up, and keep on going.

When we seek God, we will find Him. He never hides from us. When we seek God's heart above all else, we become His children with His heart pumping love and life through us and into others.

MOSES

Moses is another awesome man of God. The Bible tells us that God wanted Moses to lead the Israelites from their bondage in Egypt. After God told Moses His intent, Moses said to God, *"O Lord, I'm not very good with words. I never have been, and I'm not now, even though you have spoken to me. I get tongue-tied, and my words get tangled"* (Exodus 4:10). Whine, whine, whine. In other words, Moses said to God, "I can't do this. You're telling me to go and have an incredible teaching ministry but I—I—I'm slow to speak and I stutter."

And the Word says, *"Then the Lord became angry with Moses"* (Exodus 4:14). Why? Because Moses replied with an excuse. Essentially, he said, "NO!" God had called him and was equipping him for that calling. In Moses's natural mind, he didn't think he could be used by God. He was not an eloquent speaker and he thought he would be an embarrassment to God. Of course, that was his flesh speaking. In reality, Moses didn't want to embarrass himself. He had a poor opinion of his own abilities.

God said, *"Who makes a person's mouth? Who decides whether people speak or do not speak, hear or do not hear, see or do not see? Is it not I, the Lord? Now go! I will be with you as you speak, and I will instruct you in what to say"* (Exodus 4:11-12).

And Moses responds, *"Lord, please! Send anyone else."* And yet God used him in a miraculous way to lead the Israelites to freedom. In his later years, he didn't have to say, "I coulda shoulda…."

If God calls you to do something, He will equip you with what is required to complete your assignment. If you go off on your own without His agreement, He has no responsibility to help you or provide what you need. Remember, if He calls, He always equips.

Twenty years ago, if someone would have told me that I'd be speaking in front of a camera, I would have said the person was crazy or a false prophet. When God called me, my reaction was not positive. I thought, *I can't do that. The world says I'm dumb, stupid, ignorant, can't read, can't write. I'm a different kind of learner…and was told I'd never, ever be used of God.* That is what I believed for the majority of my life.

I could easily have said, "God, I can't," but I was reminded by the verse in the Word of God that *"I can do everything through Christ who gives me strength"* (Philippians 4:13).

JOHN MARK

Let's move on to the story about John Mark in Acts chapters 12–15. John Mark went out on the mission field with

Barnabas and Paul. When they reached Pamphylia, John Mark returned to Jerusalem. The Bible doesn't give us a reason. Perhaps he was homesick. Maybe he became ill, as many did. When he went out into the field, perhaps he realized it was a little harder than he thought it would be. When some people branch out into ministry, they quit when obstacles arise.

Little signs are posted in my house and in my office that say, "Never, never, never, never give up. Go under, go over, go through, but never give up." I'm a no-matter-what kind of a woman, and God has really used that trait for His purposes.

John Mark quit; however, he later went on other mission trips with Barnabas. He even wrote the Gospel of Mark. But I wonder what would have been written about him if he had completed that initial mission trip with Paul. Perhaps even more wonderful things would have occurred. Do you think he might have thought, *I coulda shoulda?*

THE SAMARITAN WOMAN

The Bible story in John 4 tells us about the Samaritan woman at the well. As Jesus was traveling through Samaria, He arrived at Jacob's well around noontime. Soon this woman shows up to draw water. Jesus started a conversation that would change her life forever.

Jesus said to her, "Give Me a drink." She was surprised since Jesus was a Jew. The Jewish people usually avoided the Samaritans. Then Jesus continued, "If you only knew who

I am and the gift God has for you, you would ask Me for living water." When the woman asks Him about the living water, Jesus explained that His water takes away all thirst and becomes a spring within. And she begs for some of that living water.

Scripture goes on to tell us that Jesus spoke to her for a while, telling her the things she had done in her past. He mentioned the men she had slept with out of wedlock. And when He told her He was the Messiah, she believed. Not only did she believe, she ran and told everyone in her village about Him, saying, *"He told me all that I ever did."* And many others believed too.

The point of the story is that this woman had lived a sinful life. In spite of her colorful past, Jesus loved her and was able to use her. She could have said that God couldn't use her because of her past. Instead, she believed, and God used her in a mighty way. This woman didn't have to say, "I coulda shoulda," because she did!

Understand this: God loves to forgive when we truly repent. And once we repent, God can use us in mighty ways.

ESTHER

We can't forget about a beautiful lady named Esther. She was a Jewish orphan who was raised by her cousin Mordecai. Yet despite her childhood, she was able to save the Jewish people from certain death.

Esther's story begins with King Xerxes becoming upset with his wife, Queen Vashti, and banishing her from his presence. He then began looking for another wife. Esther was one of the beautiful young virgins who were brought to the king, and he chose her as his new queen.

Although she was the queen, it was against the law for Esther to enter the king's presence without him asking for her. She couldn't say, "Honey, can we snuggle?" Esther couldn't even sleep in the same room with the king, even though they were married. In fact, it was sure death to appear in the king's inner court without an invitation, unless the king held out his scepter.

But one day a situation arose where the king's prime minister, Haman, convinced the king to let him kill all the Jews. When Esther's cousin, Mordecai, heard the decree, he tore his clothes, fasted, wept, and put on burlap—clothes of mourning—and went out into the city, crying with a loud wail (Esther 4:1).

Esther heard what had happened and she found out the details. Because she knew she had to save her people, she planned a dangerous mission. She had Mordecai gather all the Jews of Susa to fast and pray for her success. Then she prepared herself to have one night with the king that would change history.

Knowing that seeing the king without being summoned could mean her very life, she remained determined to forge ahead with her plan. Mordecai told her that she may have been placed on earth for just such a time as this (Esther 4:14). Indeed, God had her positioned in the right place at the right time to save the Jewish people.

It's so amazing how God used Esther. I know when she looked back on her life, she didn't think, *I coulda shoulda*—because she did what God called her to do, no matter the danger she faced.

PAUL

Now we come to Paul. I love Paul and how God used him. Paul (originally known as Saul of Tarsus) was a devout Jew who had persecuted and killed many Christians. One day he met Jesus on the road to Damascus, and his life was forever changed.

Although Paul was changed once he met Jesus, the Christians still feared him and his reputation. It took a while to convince them that Paul was now on the Lord's side. The Book of Acts tells us about the persecution, beatings, stonings, and problems Paul ran into when sharing his story about Jesus with others. Paul had to choose to step out of his comfort zone in order to be an effective follower of Christ (Acts 9:1-31).

The Bible never records that Paul was scared; but being human, I suspect he felt a little afraid now and then. He knew Christians were being persecuted and slaughtered. He had given the orders himself to condemn people until Jesus changed his life. Now that he was among the Christian community, he had to realize the government could now pursue and kill him. With the government on one side and the nervous Christians on the other, Paul was in a precarious position.

Yet, Paul knew he was an apostle called by God. God took this man with a horrible, murderous past and used him in such amazing ways to further His Kingdom. We can be healed, set free, and called of God; but when we pray for other people, we can be overwhelmed when we realize we are outside our comfort zone. Paul found strength and courage in Jesus. We can do the same.

Despite the many people who hurt Paul, including some in the church and the government, Paul didn't look back on his life and say, "I coulda shoulda." Instead, he did it! He did what God called him to do in life—and we continue to see lives changed centuries later because of Paul's God-inspired writings.

You've read about David, Moses, John Mark, Paul, the woman at the well, and Esther— a variety of people who were willing to sacrifice their lives to be used by God. Are you willing to sacrifice your life so God can use you? Are you willing to give up everything for Him to step into the next phase of your life?

PETER

Now I say to you that you are Peter (which means "rock"), and upon this rock I will build my church, and all the powers of hell will not conquer it (Matthew 16:18).

Here comes the apostle Peter, known as "The Rock." God said, *"Upon this rock I'll build My church."* What a strong man of great faith, right? Well, no.

When Jesus was arrested, a servant girl said to Peter, "You're one of those who followed Jesus."

"No, not me," Peter quickly said.

Later another servant saw him and said, "This man was with Jesus."

"Uh-uh, no way, I don't even know Him," he claimed.

And if that wasn't enough, Peter denied Jesus a third time just before he heard a rooster crow. Then he remembered Jesus telling him, *"You'll deny me three times before the rooster crows,"* and Peter's heart broke. (See Matthew 26:30-35; 69-75.)

But what did God do? Even though Peter denied Jesus three times, God still used him to build His church. Do you think Peter looked back and said, *"I coulda shoulda…"*? No, because God forgave him and then used him mightily.

We can deny Christ in the workplace. We can deny Christ to our neighborhood. And we can deny Christ to our family. But once we repent for that, God says, "I'm going to raise you up and use you in a mighty way."

GIDEON

Another of my favorites is Gideon. An angel of the Lord came to him and said, *"The Lord is with you, you mighty man of valor!"* And Gideon looks around, "Who me? My tribe's the weakest and I'm the least in my tribe. Oh, my Lord, how can I save Israel?" And God gave him a plan. (See Judges 6:11-16 NKJV.)

Think about that. Do you wonder if Gideon thought, *Is God a liar? Is God trying to tempt me? Is God telling me to do something knowing I'll fail?* No, God's not like that. He doesn't see our past, He sees our future. He sees our present, but He wants our present to turn around. When you understand the call of God on your life, even if you feel like a Gideon, God will use you in a mighty way. I know Gideon didn't review his life and say, *"I coulda shoulda…."*

AIMEE SEMPLE MCPHERSON

A modern-day woman I really like and admire is Aimee Semple McPherson. I thank God for her for so many reasons. Do you know that before Aimee, women in the church weren't allowed to cut their hair or wear makeup? She opened that door for us. She's now deceased, but Aimee was an awesome woman of God with an extremely strong call of God on her life. Aimee was called to tell the world about Jesus, and she traveled as much as possible. Aimee was both widowed and divorced. She was kicked out of the church— because she was divorced and because she was a woman who wanted to minister to the people who needed to hear about Jesus.

What would you do if something like that happened to you? Would you quit following your calling, thinking, "Well, they won't let me minister here because I'm a woman. They won't let me minister there because I'm divorced." What's your excuse?

I imagine Aimee thought, *I'm not going to sit here and do nothing. I'll begin my own denomination.* She didn't give up in failure. Instead, she started the Foursquare Gospel Church, which, at this point, is the largest growing denomination in the world today. How awesome is that? This church came about because of one woman's persecution. Man told her she couldn't. But God said, "Yes, you can. With Me, you can do anything."

JOAN

How can I, Joan Hunter, travel the world? God gave me a plan.

How can you do what He's called you to do? God will give you His plan specifically designed for you.

Many years ago, I worked at a car dealership which was and is an amazing company in the Dallas-Fort Worth area. It was one of the best things that ever happened to me. At the time, I had low self-esteem. I couldn't do anything because I had been told repeatedly that I'd never be able to hold a job. But I not only got the job, I learned a lot and received the highest awards and accolades available in the company. I served there for ten years.

The dealership also offered body work services, and one day I asked, "May I have a rearview mirror?" There were lots of mirrors in the body shop, so the answer was, "Sure." Every car has to have a rearview mirror. It is a safety device.

However, when driving down the road, if you are constantly looking in the rearview mirror, you will run into something in front of you. That mirror is for glancing into occasionally while driving forward into your future.

Oftentimes, though, people concentrate on their past instead of focusing on their future. They continually live in the past, thinking of all the times they let God down. They think about the *coulda's* and *shoulda's* of their lives and how they've denied Christ and backslid into sin. They falsely believe there is no way God would ever use them.

Be assured, there is nothing wrong with thinking about your past and learning from it, but God wants you to focus on your future. Choose your path for tomorrow. Put God's will in front of you as your goal for life.

I look back on my life and say, "I'm so not the same person I used to be." I look at my future and think, "I'm a woman after God's own heart. May He use me for His purposes."

Every person must choose to rise up and meet the call of God on their life. God must get very tired of hearing His children's whining and excuses.

How does a mother feel when she tells her children, "Make your beds," and they just keep on playing? Every mother can relate to this scenario. "I love your eyes, Mommy," one child might say to distract mother's frustration. Or something else catches their attention and the beds remain unmade. Another may say, "I'll go make you some breakfast," or they bring her a flower and a kiss—but they still haven't made their beds.

God wants us to start off our day speaking to Him and asking for His guidance, the same way some of us automatically make the bed when we get up in the morning. He wants us to wake up in the morning with an attitude of obedience ready to follow His instructions for the day.

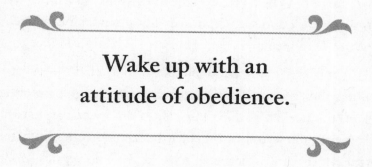

Wake up with an attitude of obedience.

God uses me in an incredible way in services around the world. But what is so awesome is that I can walk up to people in an airport and God can heal someone through me whose body is bent over, wracked with pain. This person has absolutely no idea who Joan Hunter is—yet I see him or her walk away, healed in the name of Jesus, with no pain or trouble moving. As they leave, I hear them say, "I don't even know her name. I just remember the name Jesus!"

When I go to the grocery store, a superstore, anyplace, I love it when God heals others through me. He can do the same for you and through you. Let Him use you to do His work. Make sure those you minister to know that Jesus is doing the healing. They will remember the name of Jesus, even if they don't know your name.

YOU

What has God called you to do? It's so important that you understand the call of God on your life, so you don't end up with regret. When you're eighty years old, you don't want to think back and say, "Man, I really shoulda done that," or "Wow, I coulda done that!"

Nowadays many people make a "bucket list"—a list of things they want to do or places they want to go before they "kick the bucket." I don't put things on my bucket list that I'm never going to do so that my bucket won't be full before I kick it. I want to leave this world with no regrets, no, "I couldas or shouldas…." to bother me.

I remember one time when some people with cancer said, "I just want to live long enough to go to one of Charles and Frances Hunter's meetings." They didn't attend to receive healing, but just to meet Mom and Dad, before they died.

What are you confessing out of your mouth? "God will never use me. I'm too old, too young, too fat, too skinny, married, not married, have children, or don't have children?" God wants all those excuses thrown out the window. Get them out of your vocabulary. He just wants to use *you*— if you're willing. And if you let Him minister through you to others, your life will be an amazing journey.

Be willing to simply pray, "Father God, use me. I repent for any of my excuses. I repent for denying Your power through me. I don't want to move into the category of coulda and shoulda or I wish I had. I want to live a life of no regrets from this moment on. In Jesus' name. Amen."

That said, God will use you in a mighty way!

Chapter 2

DREAMS OF DESTINY

*D*o you have unfulfilled dreams? God put it on my heart to tell you about seeing your dreams come to pass.

We've seen and experienced a lot of glory through our ministry. And we have seen a lot of miracles. For example, a woman who came to one of our services wasn't able to stand. We prayed for her in the afternoon—and she stood during our evening worship service—that's a miracle! The woman's dream was to be able to walk. She came to Texas from Canada through sheer determination. She returned home healed, in Jesus' name. I have a video of her walking. Praise the Lord, her dream was fulfilled!

A few years ago, God asked me, "How badly do you want it?"

Now, *it* can be anything. *It* can be marriage, *it* can be money, *it* can be success, *it* can be ministry, *it* can be so many things—but how badly do I want "*it*"? His question made me stop and think about *it*.

What are you willing to do to get *it*—to live your dream or to fulfill your destiny?

Some people are willing to do whatever they can to get *it*. Sometimes, the situation might be just slightly off so they have to push down the door to get *it*. You need to be determined about fulfilling your dreams; but if the door is too hard to push, back off. There's another door coming. And more than likely, the correct door is a better, easier door, an open door waiting right in front of you. God's timing is important.

WAITING

My number-three daughter, Melody Barker, has written a book titled, *While You Are Waiting: How to Make the Most of Where You Are*. It's about what to do while you're waiting for *it*—your miracle to manifest, your dream to come to pass. In her book, she wrote about a situation that happened to her. She started griping, complaining, and was mad at everybody. At the time, I often thought and said, "Where did my sweet Melody go?"

Well, Melody had a physical problem, but through a series of circumstances, she was healed. Praise God! God spoke to her and said, "You're waiting, but you're not waiting well." Realize that God will rebuke you because He loves you.

God told Melody, "When you learn to wait well, then what you've been waiting for will come." So, Melody's book is about learning to wait well, no matter what it is—a career promotion, opportunity in ministry, whatever. It's about having peace in all that God's called you to do, and calmly waiting for His perfect timing.

But that doesn't mean you just sit back and wait for *it* to happen. The Word says, *"But those who wait on the Lord shall renew their strength..."* (Isaiah 40:31 NKJV). So, what does that mean? Sit down in a chair and wait? Tell that to your wait-ress, "Just sit down and wait." No, you serve. While you are waiting, you serve.

For example, when you volunteer to do what you can to help my friend David Herzog,[1] who experiences and writes extensively about God's glory, trust me, more glory is going to go home with you every time. When you honor somebody like David, you will walk in greater glory than you've ever walked in before.

Likewise, when you serve somebody like Doug Addison,[2] you will also walk in the prophetic. When you serve with someone like me,[3] you will walk in incredible anointing where healing is concerned. Not that the others don't all have the gift of healing, but I believe I have a supernatural anointing for healing which manifests immediately on the spot. God has blessed me with this gift—and I am honored to walk it out in my daily life.

Each of us has a specific supernatural gift that we walk in. Watch for how He wants to use you.

If you are in need of healing, you don't always have to learn to wait well for it to happen. I want you to get it now—hallelujah!

GET RID OF THE JUNK

There are things that can block your healing. I encourage you to sincerely ask God, "If there's anything in my heart that's not of You, Lord, show me. What's done in darkness, God, let it be revealed in the light" (see 1 Corinthians 4:5).

Because Jesus is coming back for a church without spot or wrinkle and for people without a bunch of junk in their hearts, we need to clean out and clean up. For example, if so-and-so, who hurt you last year or fifty years ago, were to walk into the room, is your first urge to yell, throw up, leave, or whatever? If you think you would have any of those reactions, you haven't forgiven the person.

However, the Word doesn't say you have to be best pals and go out to eat together once a week and text each other constantly. No. Your forgiveness must be sincere, but it doesn't have to be overly compensating.

Walking out your forgiveness, in my opinion, makes you look younger—you no longer have the junk showing up on your face and showing in your attitude. You won't carry the heaviness in your heart. And so, you look younger. Of course, you can get a face peel or plastic surgery; but you know what? The best thing to do is get your heart healed by forgiving anyone who has hurt you.

About eighteen years ago, my heart was so damaged that the doctors gave me no hope for recovering from breast cancer. My CPA gave me no hope financially. And the counselor told me, "You'll never, ever get over all this stuff that has happened to you."

And I thought, *Well, that doesn't line up with God's Word, the Bible.* So, I went to three different Spirit-filled counselors. They all said the same thing. Please don't misunderstand me, I'm all for counselors, but what happened to me was so devastating that they didn't give me any hope. I only had a faithful, loving God to turn to for help, hope, and my future.

Long story short, my heart was healed, I became free of any unforgiveness, betrayal, abandonment, worry, the whole bit. Supernaturally, I was healed of breast cancer. My finances were healed, and *"I ain't po' no more! Hallelujah! Glory to God and amen!"*

God wants to meet you where you are. He wants to heal you—in your body, your mind, your soul, your spirit, and your finances. So, you can say, "I ain't po' no more! Hallelujah! Hallelujah!"

DEAD DREAMS

One evening, as I was praying before a worship service, God said to me, "Many of those who are coming tonight have dead dreams." Some of the worshipers had just flat out given up on their dreams for their future. That service happened to be on Resurrection Sunday.

In the Bible, it is obvious that Jesus' followers were distraught after His crucifixion. They had waited so long for the Messiah. Once He had arrived, they learned from Him, they trusted Him, and they were fully devoted to Him. Then their Savior died. Their dreams and destiny seemed to die with Him. They couldn't comprehend how He would come back to life. The church died that day.

But—on the third day…Jesus and the church were resurrected. Today, the church has a risen Savior. Dreams can now flourish, and visions come true! Now is the time and the season. God says, "This is a day when your dreams are going to come to life again." God certainly did not give you a dream in order to punish you. He gives only good plans and good gifts from above designed specifically for your health and joy (see Jeremiah 29:11; James 1:17; Romans 8:28).

I have two friends who have had very devastating situations in the past few years and their dreams are yet to come to pass. Roadblocks and many circumstances stand in the way of the fulfillment of their dream. Yet, they trust God and have faith in His plan and timing.

Everyone has to face obstructions that stop us from accomplishing what God has called us to do. When that happens, we need to figure out what the problem is, why it is, what's going on, and what steps to take to move the roadblock out of the way. Then we need to actually take those steps and focus on the future.

THE NEED TO KNOW

One spring I was invited to speak at a women's conference, Women on the Frontlines in Chicago. As I was getting ready to go up front and minister, I heard, "You want to know what the devil thinks of you?"

"Not really," I replied, but I knew I was hearing the voice of God, so I figured He wanted me to know. As I prayed, I again heard His voice, "Do you want to know what the devil thinks of you?"

"I really, really don't care. I don't care, truly, I don't care," I said. So even though I knew God was speaking to me, I really didn't care what the devil thought of me. But I realized that God wanted me to know.

Then God said, "The devil says, 'You are absolutely amazing. You are so beautiful or handsome. You are so gifted that there's nothing you can do wrong and everything you put your hand to is going to prosper. You're going to come up with some witty inventions that are going to bring millions into the Kingdom of God. You have a brilliant mind and have a lot of books in you. You will be able to teach and travel and sing, whatever your dream may be. God is going to raise you up to be an icon all around the world, an example for many. There's such a strong call on your life, and God will give you incredible, phenomenal revelations—and I'm going to do whatever I can do to keep you from your calling!'"

That was a lot to absorb and I knew God wanted me to use that wisdom with the audience during the service. So, during the worship service, I asked a woman to come forward and sit at the end of the front row. I told her she could move back to her seat in a few minutes. Then I said, "I'm going to speak over this woman what the devil thinks of her. Some of you will relate to everything I'm saying. Some of you will relate to the majority of what I'm going to say. And the only difference will be if you are a female compared to a male. Now pay attention: if God can use this person, He can use anybody, even me."

There was a holy hush over the people in the service. I thought, Hmm, maybe that's why the devil's been fighting me, so I could get to where I am today—where I need to be. Go figure.

The devil is trying to blow your dreams to pieces. Just like Humpty Dumpy fell off the wall and broke into a million pieces, all the king's horses and all the king's men couldn't put him back together again. And that's exactly what happened to me—family, friends, teachers, doctors, and even Christian counselors told me I'd never be able to put the pieces of my life back together again. While attending school, the enemy tried to shut me up by telling me I was dumb, stupid, ignorant and I would never amount to anything or even keep a job.

Yet now I'm president of Joan Hunter Ministries and known worldwide. We serve a great God!

DREAMS REQUIRE ACTION

During a trip to Israel, I was reminded of Hannah in the Bible. Hannah wanted a baby so badly. She went into the temple and cried, screaming out to God. This is the first time the Bible mentions that a woman prayed to God—women just didn't do that back then. There are some places even today where women aren't allowed to pray out loud. But we can always pray directly to God in our spirits.

When the temple rabbi saw Hannah, he thought she was drunk because she was mourning so much for the child she was unable to have.

Sometimes because of our unrealized dreams and promises, we get to the point where we just cry and sob. We think our dream has died. Other people may even think we are drunk because we are so sad and inconsolable.

But what happens to Hannah? The rabbi tells her to go home and prepare for her child. (See First Samuel 1.) So, Hannah goes home and sits in her rocking chair. Will she see her dream come to pass while rocking away in her chair? Of course not. She must put some action to it. Need some help on that one? Hannah had to go home and do her part to see that miracle manifested. She said to her husband, "I've just been to the temple, honey. Let's work on our dream together." Consequently, she had three daughters and two sons, one of which was Samuel. Glory to God!

Take notice—your dreams require action!

If you need a financial miracle, what are you supposed to do? Give. That doesn't seem to make any sense, but God doesn't have to make sense to us. His ways are much different from our ways:

"My thoughts are nothing like your thoughts," says the Lord. "And my ways are far beyond anything you could imagine. For just as the heavens are higher than the earth, so my ways are higher than your ways and my thoughts higher than your thoughts" (Isaiah 55:8-9).

God makes miracles happen. If you could figure it out on your own, you wouldn't need God to be involved. Believe God for a supernatural financial breakthrough and keep praying. But if you keep watching CNN, "Constant Negative News," your faith for financial breakthrough will go right out the window.

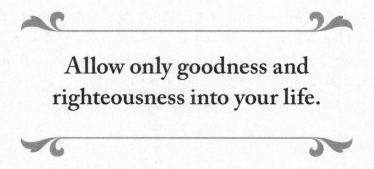

Allow only goodness and righteousness into your life.

We have to get to the point where we only allow the good into our lives. No longer should we have to need Holy Ghost Q-tips to clean out our ears to hear His voice and swabs to clean our spirits of death, doubt, unbelief, and all kinds of other junk we tend to keep in that space between our ears and in our hearts.

Seriously, what are your dreams?

"Oh, my dream is to open a painting and remodeling business."

"Have you read any books about starting a business? Do you know the difference between the variety of paints? How much remodeling experience do you have?"

"Hmmm…well…no, no, and none."

I'm exaggerating, but I want you to get the point. I speak very simply, sometimes so simply that the point may not dawn on you until a couple of days later, but that's okay. If you're believing in God for an incredible painting ministry and you don't even have a paintbrush, don't expect Him to carry you toward your dream by Himself. You have a significant role to play in your own destiny.

"Well, I'd like this room a real pretty blue." Or pink. Blush or bashful? If you've ever seen the movie *Steel Magnolias,* you know exactly what I mean. It's pink. No, it's blush and bashful. You have to learn colors and hues. Well, blue is blue, right? No. There are dozens of shades of blue, more than any other color.

If you want to paint, the Word says, *"Work hard so you can present yourself to God and receive his approval. Be a good worker, one who does not need to be ashamed and who correctly explains the word of truth"* (2 Timothy 2:15). And, *"Many are called, but few are chosen"* (Matthew 22:14).

Let me rephrase that second Scripture verse: "Many are called but few *choose.*"

BE EAGER TO LEARN

Everyone who attends my Complete Healing School is called to the healing ministry—and to the prophetic realm as well. The Word says, *"Be eager to prophesy"* (1 Corinthians 14:39). Being eager means yearning to learn how to hear His voice, and then repeat what He wants to be heard through you to others.

Many times, when I've prophesied over someone from the platform, the person looks over at their friend and says something like, "I didn't tell her anything about that. I never said a word to her!" The person is stunned because what I prophesied is so right on. All I'm doing is hearing from God and repeating it to the person who needs to hear what He has to say.

Students in my schools are called to cast out devils. They are taught not to be afraid to stand strong against the wiles of the enemy. After all, they're not in a good place if they are scared to cast out devils. The devil is afraid of me. He should be afraid of you, too! We have to make the devil tremble. And not just by purpose but by being—being warriors for God who put our enemy in his place and kick him out of our lives.

IDENTIFY YOUR DREAM

What dream did God put in your heart?

"Oh, my dream? To own a business...but this isn't a good time."

Says who? You've prolonged it, postponed it, and procrastinated long enough. Pregnancy is only nine months, but there's a serious problem if you carry a baby for eighteen months. A problem with the mother, with the doctor, and with the baby. But you may be eighteen *years* pregnant with your dream. I say it is time to birth that dream. It's time to birth what God has called you to do. And I pray this book and the Holy Spirit's nudging will impress upon you the urgency to begin your journey toward your destiny.

A friend of mine went through a really hard time about two years ago. A hard time is an understatement. She moved into our home and lived with us for about ten months. She calls our home the Hunters' House of Healing because she came to our home and was healed.

I introduced her to a man, for whom she now works, and so forth and so on, and things have spiraled her into a good place in her life. Sometimes people need a safe place where they can go to be healed. Now my friend has an awesome new apartment right down the street from us—and she's so very excited. She is living her dream—one of them. There are still a couple more dreams that she has, and we are all sure that each one will come to pass. She is so fulfilled right now that she's like a kid in a candy store.

That's what God wants for you too. He wants you to be so filled and fulfilled that you feel like you're living in a candy store. But His treats are not fattening and not bad for your teeth. It's Heaven on earth. I've heard prophetess Kat Kerr say that "Jesus likes a lot of desserts." Today, I know that my mom is truly in Heaven—eating all the desserts she loves and not gaining any weight.

My mom had a printing company. I grew up in the business and on a daily basis I use my background in printing in my ministry. When printing books and other publications, getting the right paper is important—there are lots of details that go into producing and presenting quality printed materials. "I want this design, I want this brochure. I need seventy-pound paper, I need twenty-pound." Or, "I want this on crump card, I want this finish, etc." I know all that stuff because of what I learned decades ago. I was three years of age when I started helping my mom in her business. At that point, I just licked stamps, but it got me started in the printing business.

God wants to use your past, too. But you may be wondering, *I don't even want to think about my past, let alone use any of it.* I didn't say to *think* about your past, I said God wants to *use* your past. God has given you giftings that you've already used, maybe not for His glory. Now He wants you to identify the gifts He gave to you so He can turn them around for His glory.

TAMING THE PAST

The Bible tells us that Mary Magdalene had seven demons cast out of her (Mark 16:9). Do you think being possessed was her dream? I'm sure it was not. This woman's dream was to be a follower of Jesus. Who was the first person Jesus appeared to after He arose to life on the third day after His crucifixion? Mary Magdalene. Her dream was truly fulfilled.

And there's David and Goliath. When David volunteered to kill Goliath, no one believed he would succeed. His past experience was taking care of the sheep for his family. How could his past help him face the giant? According to First Samuel 17, David had already killed a lion and a bear that had tried to destroy the flock. David had learned how to handle wild beasts. He was strong, prepared, and he knew how to use his slingshot.

God used David's past to launch him into his future. Killing the lion and the bear prepared him for killing Goliath, the Philistine giant determined to destroy the Israelites. When none of the brave, strong soldiers would fight Goliath, young David silenced the giant with only one stone from his slingshot.

God will use your past to launch you into your future.

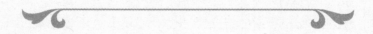

About my past I could have said, "Well, the printing business was before I was saved, so I can't do that. I shouldn't use that knowledge." No. That's not the way God works. He uses all things for our betterment if we trust Him. I have written many books that have been published and my prior printing business expertise helped during the process. Yes, it was part of the past, but it's part of who I am today.

The same is true for you. God wants to use your brain. He wants to use your past experiences. He wants to use all of that to help you in your future. A future that you have never, ever thought possible.

We have to stop listening to the enemy. He's trying to talk us out of what God wants and he's really doing a good job. We need to say, "Back off! Go away, because I'm going to do what God's called me to do!" We must be strong and determined in staying on the path and going in the direction where God is leading us.

STEPPING INTO YOUR FUTURE

God gave me a dream. The dream He gave me isn't like a carrot dangling in front of me that I would never, ever reach. God gave me a dream that I could accomplish. I could live that dream and then dream again and again and have even bigger dreams. God helped me grab hold of each one and accomplish each purpose He designed just for me. I will never stop dreaming something new and exciting.

He has dreams designed for you too. All you need to do is reach out, keep moving forward, and your dreams will become your destiny fulfilled.

We all tend to limit God. I did. Years ago, there's no way I would have ever dreamed of having a microphone in my hand, much less around my ear, or that I would have numerous books published.

You have no idea what miracles God has brought into my life. Speaking in front of people? No, not in my dreams of twenty years ago. Having people compare me to Frances Hunter? No, I'll never be Frances Hunter. I'm a lot like her because she's my mom, but I'm Joan Hunter. I have my own ministry now—thanks to God fulfilling His dreams for me.

What is in your heart that God is trying to get out? What have you been keeping to yourself that you could be giving away? If you feel like you don't have any giftings, start by being a church or ministry greeter and a hugger. Who doesn't need a hug? Often the only hug a person receives is at church each week. Make someone's day—share a hug! If hugging isn't your style, say something nice to people you meet. It could be something as simple as, "Hi! Have a nice day" or "What a great shirt!" or "Those shoes are awesome!" You get the idea.

Hugs, sincere compliments, taking a meal to someone who is ill—there are so many little things you can do to help brighten someone else's day and will give you warm fuzzy feelings inside at the same time. You have the ability to wipe away the clouds in someone's day.

However, please be careful when talking to someone of the opposite sex. Don't let your enthusiasm to brighten someone's day give the person the wrong impression. I recommend that females interact with females and males with males so no misunderstandings happen. For instance, if a man said to a woman, "You have really pretty eyes," he may give the woman an entirely wrong impression of what he meant by that compliment.

REACHING OUT—OF YOUR COMFORT ZONE

Now a serious question, how do you feel after you give a hug or a compliment or receive a hug or compliment? It feels great, right? Giving and receiving both feel great. Isn't that amazing?

One thing I really like to do is carry a few five-dollar bills in my pocket. When I'm in the airport and I see somebody cleaning the toilets, I give the woman a five. I doubt that when she was a little girl, she dreamed of cleaning toilets. But yet I surely do appreciate the clean restrooms. I always say, "Thank you," and if I have a five, I'll give it to her.

"You're giving me money?" is the usual response.

I smile and say, "Yeah, I appreciate what you do. I know this probably isn't your dream job, but a clean restroom makes my life better. Thanks!"

Compliment someone today. If you don't give money, that's okay. All of a sudden, the person will take pride in their work. Tell your trash collector, "Thanks! I'm so glad you come and pick up my garbage twice a week. I really appreciate the work you do."

When you give sincere compliments, you will light up a person's life. You give them hope. You make them feel appreciated. And you both feel better.

Where do you keep your dreams? Inside a little safe with a combination or lock? Are they locked away so you can't easily access them? God has given me the key, the combination, and I am unlocking your dreams, in Jesus' name.

Today you are going to have a breakthrough. You're going to open that safe and access your dreams. If your dream is to do great things for God prophetically, believe that you're going to lay hands on the sick and see them recover. You're going to walk up to a stranger and prophesy. You may hear God telling you to say, "God's called you, and I see you having a baby." You will most likely be surprised at the words He tells you to share with others. Your words will change someone's life.

Whatever your dream is, unlock it, and see it fulfilled. I want to encourage you—this is the time and the season for your dreams to become unlocked, to be unleashed, and for you to walk them out of your mind and into your life— make them real. Then dream again and again.

God gave a dream to my friend about pieces of paper with glue on one end. She didn't take the dream seriously— she threw out the dream. Now somebody else is making millions of dollars off her idea for Post-It notes.

If you don't have a dream right now, don't be discouraged. God will give you a dream so you can do what He's called you to do, so you can open the windows of Heaven in your life. You will be able to fund the Kingdom of God with millions of dollars, if that is truly His dream for you and you are willing to take the necessary action to make it happen.

Unleash your dream— make it real.

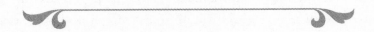

I feel it is imminent—potentially very soon—that there will be a release, a transference of finances. A great transference of wealth; not a hundred dollars or a hundred thousand dollars. I'm talking about millions and millions. I believe that wealth will be poured out into ministries and churches and people who will do something good with all those financial resources.

This is your time, this is your season, because the need is greater than ever. I want to stir your spirit to dream—and dream again. Right now, I'd like to pray for you:

> *Father, right now in the precious name of Jesus,
> I send the word of a breakthrough anointing, the
> breakthrough angel right now, in Jesus' name, to
> burst open whatever container that has kept this
> reader's dreams and visions locked away for far
> too long. Open this person's heart and spirit to
> hear directly from You how to make their dream
> a reality—dream after dream after dream.
> Father, You have all keys, and I believe, as
> does the reader, that Your key is unlocking their*

dream. It is being released right now in Jesus' name. Hallelujah!

GOD—THE DREAM RELEASER

Your dream is now being released to you. I'm speaking to greater dreams, greater visions than you have ever experienced in your entire life. You will walk out your dreams. In Jesus' name, I'm speaking resurrection life, resurrection of your dreams, resurrection breakthrough, resurrection of self-doubt and negative self-talk. You will maintain a positive attitude and cut off words that stifle God's plan. I'm speaking to your dream—that it will come to pass for greater breakthrough. The dreams that you have dreamed before are going to come to pass, and then you're going to dream more.

And what you've been dreaming for is nothing compared to what your next set of dreams will be. You will see the manifestation of His power in and through you, through the prophetic and through healing. It will be like, "Wow, all I did was say 'Yes' and I just made a hundred thousand dollars on that deal. That's got to be God!"

You've seen your dreams in your spirit, but now it's time that you see them in the natural. Let's pray together:

> *Father, right now in the name of Jesus, I speak resurrection power for this reader's dreams. I speak to their dreams to live again, live again, live again (notice three times). On the third, they're going to be raised from the dead,*

they're going to come to fruition like they never thought possible.

Father, I pray in Jesus' name, Your power will fall and doors will fly open. Father, I thank You right now for jobs, promotions, and open doors for ministry will be set before this reader that have never even been thought about. Perhaps, Lord, you have in mind a healing room in their home that is open to the neighborhood. Hallelujah!

You may be thinking, Well, I can't do that.

Shut your mouth! Quit talking yourself out of the glory. Quit talking yourself out of the abundance of God's bounty.

Well, I don't deserve…

Shut your mouth!

Well, there's already a prophetic ministry, why should I start one?

Because God wants you to.

There's already a book about this.

So what? God wants you to write another one.

There are already numerous painting businesses.

But yours is going to be the best.

During a class at my school, I had a word for someone; God called the person to start a newspaper. Even though that doesn't make sense because everything is online, this newspaper could be online too. And, this person is to start a newspaper that shares only the truth. Yes! She wants to call it *Re-News*. God's already put the dream in her heart, "Wow, I'd love to start a newspaper!"

God told her, "Now's the time because people are tired of all the junk."

Others in class received a word including people's dreams to be massage therapists and hairstylists, but they had been talked out of reaching those dreams over the years.

Maybe you've been talked out of your dream. Resurrect it—it's time to walk out your dream starting today. Too many dreams have been stolen. Reclaim them, bring them back into your life's journey, in Jesus' name. Hallelujah!

What is your dream of destiny?

Let God help you fulfill it. Start today.

ENDNOTES

1. For more information about David Herzog's ministry, visit https://thegloryzone.org/.

2. For more information about Doug Addison's ministry, visit https://dougaddison.com/.

3. For more information about my ministries, visit https://joanhunter.org/.

Chapter 3

LABELS—DESTRUCTIVE OR CONSTRUCTIVE

As mentioned in Chapter 1, I had a job at a car dealer-ship for ten years. Before moving on, I won all the awards available at that business. I was determined to be the best Christian example anyone could ever be. The boss told me, "You're the only Christian we've ever been willing to hire because it was so obvious that you have such a strong faith."

That was a really sad statement, as the business consisted of eighteen car dealerships and hundreds of employees. The comment reminded me that I may be the only Christian some people ever know or meet. We must be good examples of our good and faithful Savior.

My point is, until I was about twenty-seven years of age, I lived with all the denigrating statements made about me. In school I didn't apply myself, I just sat there. If I was good, they passed me to the next grade. I was never encouraged to study. My mom didn't say that I was stupid, she just accepted it as fact and never encouraged me or challenged me to do anything. Which, again, is very sad.

I'm a cognitive learner, which back then was considered "retarded." I learn differently—but I can learn. Not everybody can, but I can. Once I figured out how to study, I continued to acquire knowledge. By then, though, I had unfortunately learned to live with the labels "stupid," "ignorant," etc.

Then in the year 2000, I was labeled, "Divorced." Along with that word, I heard, "You will never be used of God again. You can't minister in the pulpit. You're an abomination to your parents, not to mention God."

Divorced from a pastor Yes. Divorced from an evangelist. Yes. Divorced from the father of my children. Yes. But he was living a double life as a homosexual. I had all the biblical reasons for divorce, but I stayed with him several years longer because of an unhealthy codependency. And I believe that all the worry and everything associated with this bad relationship is what brought on my cancer.

I was told to renounce the soul ties with my husband. So I renounced the soul ties and didn't feel anything different. Then two years later I learned about "covenant." When I married him, I went into covenant with him, not a soul tie. So, I renounced the covenant I made with him and things changed. You see, for those first two years after the divorce, I was still in covenant with everything he was doing, which meant I was participating in that sin.

COMPLETELY FREE

If you are in covenant with someone, you may at times feel sort of yucky or strange. Well, that feeling could be from a previous partner doing something unrighteous. When you get the revelation of that, it may affect your spirit. The point is, after I renounced the covenant I had with my ex-husband, I was completely free! Including being healed supernaturally of breast cancer, supernaturally receiving financially blessing, and becoming supernaturally clean in my mind. It was absolutely amazing!

The next step after the divorce was to figure out who in the world Joan was. I had always been the child of Charles and Frances Hunter, a wife, a mother, and co-pastor of the church. Then I lost it all—parents, husband, kids moved out—all within a month. On top of that, I lost my health. All my dreams were gone.

I had always wanted to co-pastor a church and always wanted to be married, so I pretty much married the first guy I ever dated. Then in the blink of an eye, everything was stripped from me. The kids were old enough, so they moved out. And I had nothing but the big dogs and five fish. I finally realized that it was time to reclaim what the enemy had stolen.

You may be able to relate to my situation.

We need to reclaim our dreams! We need to call them back. We need to speak to those dreams. Maybe it's been so long that we don't even remember what those dreams are. But God will bring them back to you. When He does, write them on a sheet of paper, and say, "Father, Your Word says to remind You, so I'm reminding you of this dream that you gave me. I'm reminding you that I want to make this dream a reality." (See Isaiah 43:26.)

RENOUNCING LABELS

The following is a tremendous revelation that I recently received regarding labels. After the divorce I felt as if a heavy chain was around my neck because of all the baggage it came with. The divorce wasn't something that I wanted, yet it was inevitable because of the circumstances. When I finally got hold of the reality of it all, I yanked off that chain and declared that I was not going to be known or labeled as the "divorced woman," the "victim," "stupid," or someone who was less than whole.

In the spirit realm, our hearts are labeled by God. His label for us—My beloved child. The more labels we allow to seep into our minds, the more distracted we become from the label God has given us in our hearts.

Writing down your dreams will help keep you focused on the right label—your God-destined label of being His child and able to follow through with His design for your life. Keeping your dreams alive is your most important job in life. Dream big!

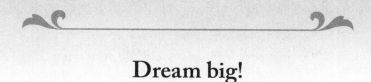

Dream big!

I dream about all the wonderful, new, and exciting adventures that God has for me. I dream about all the doors He continues to open for me. And I acknowledge all the blessings He has showered me with over the years while making those dreams come true. Because I have faith in His will for me, I see signs, wonders, and miracles wherever I go. People are set free, healed, and delivered from all sorts of trauma and desperation, depression and hopelessness.

First, we must renounce all the wrong labels that the world has assigned to us. No matter who told us this or that, we must renounce, reject all the labels that may hold us back from our identity—a chosen, loved child of God who is healed and whole.

A BIBLICAL EXAMPLE

Saul was one of the witnesses, and he agreed completely with the killing of Stephen. A great wave of persecution began that day, sweeping over the church in Jerusalem; and all the believers except the apostles were scattered through the regions of Judea and Samaria. (Some devout men

> *came and buried Stephen with great mourning.)*
> *But Saul was going everywhere to destroy the*
> *church. He went from house to house, dragging out*
> *both men and women to throw them into prison*
> (Acts 8:1-3).

Saul was a zealot. He fiercely believed in his mission to root out and destroy Christians, thinking they were wrong about Jesus being the Messiah. His label as a zealot was true at the time of Stephen's death by stoning. Paul was focused on his mission: *"Meanwhile, Saul was uttering threats with every breath and was eager to kill the Lord's followers..."* (Acts 9:1).

But the Lord had a more important mission for Saul, one that would bring many millions to the saving gospel of Jesus as Lord and Savior. The Lord enlisted Ananias to help Saul see the light of the Spirit. But because of Saul's label as a zealot, Ananias was afraid to obey the Lord:

> *"But Lord," exclaimed Ananias, "I've heard*
> *many people talk about the terrible things this*
> *man has done to the believers in Jerusalem!*
> *And he is authorized by the leading priests to*
> *arrest everyone who calls upon your name"*
> (Acts 9:13-14).

The Lord was insistent, so Ananias obeyed and went to visit Saul:

> *So Ananias went and found Saul. He laid his hands on him and said, "Brother Saul, the Lord Jesus, who appeared to you on the road, has sent me so that you might regain your sight and be filled with the Holy Spirit." Instantly something like scales fell from Saul's eyes, and he regained his sight. Then he got up and was baptized. Afterward he ate some food and regained his strength* (Acts 9:17-19).

Saul's life was changed—he was no longer the man he used to be. He was filled with the Holy Spirit and became a champion for Jesus the Messiah.

> *And immediately he* [Saul] *began preaching about Jesus in the synagogues, saying, "He is indeed the Son of God!" All who heard him were amazed. "Isn't this the same man who caused such devastation among Jesus' followers in Jerusalem?" they asked. "And didn't he come here to arrest them and take them in chains to the leading priests?" Saul's preaching became more and more powerful, and the Jews in Damascus couldn't refute his proofs that Jesus was indeed the Messiah* (Acts 9:20-22).

Now Saul renounced his old label. He chose one that suited his new status as a believer of the Lord Jesus. People didn't understand. And people may not understand your new label—but nonetheless, you are a child of God, a believer, a dreamer of dreams, a person of destiny. Your label suits you!

During Saul's first missionary journey, he met a sorcerer who was no match for him:

> *Saul, also known as Paul, was filled with the Holy Spirit, and he looked the sorcerer in the eye. Then he said, "You son of the devil, full of every sort of deceit and fraud, and enemy of all that is good! Will you never stop perverting the true ways of the Lord? Watch now, for the Lord has laid his hand of punishment upon you, and you will be struck blind. You will not see the sunlight for some time." Instantly mist and darkness came over the man's eyes, and he began groping around begging for someone to take his hand and lead him. When the governor saw what had happened, he became a believer, for he was astonished at the teaching about the Lord* (Acts 13:9-12).

From this verse forward throughout the New Testament, Saul was known as Paul. His label and his name changed to reflect his new self—his new mission in Christ. Paul wrote most of the New Testament. His writings have affected millions and millions of people worldwide for multiple centuries. Had he not been open to God's plan for his life, the world would be in a dismal state.

He overcame his worldly label and accepted his godly label—and changed the world by proclaiming Jesus as Lord.

Paul knew exactly who he was in Christ. He wrote to the church in Philippi:

> *I press on to possess that perfection for which Christ Jesus first possessed me. No, dear brothers and sisters, I have not achieved it, but I focus on this one thing:* **Forgetting the past and looking forward** *to what lies ahead, I press on to reach the end of the race and receive the heavenly prize for which God, through Christ Jesus, is calling us* (Philippians 3:12-14).

Paul had to forget his past—his murderous past—so he could focus on the future. His new desire was to positively affect the future for himself and many others.

Many people, maybe even you, drag around the past like a ball and chain strapped around your leg, keeping you from running toward an exciting future. Wrapped around that ball and chain are all the labels you have been called over the years. Let me tell you right know that Jesus is the key to unlocking whatever is holding you back. His shed blood can wash away whatever labels have been tainting your life. You must forget your past in order to do what God called you to do.

God gave Paul incredible love for people. Because Paul knew their very lives depended on knowing God through Jesus, he sat down and penned letters to churches, his spiritual son Timothy, and others. These are all contained in the Bible—God's love letter to all people who choose to believe.

Paul chose to forget what was behind him and he pressed on to become everything God called him to do.

A PRESIDENTIAL EXAMPLE

Abraham Lincoln is considered one the best presidents in American history. Although he is known as the president who destroyed slavery, many don't realize the failure labels he experienced during his lifetime before his God-given vision was made a reality. He was labeled a failure for:

- Losing his job

- Being defeated twice for a legislature position

- Failing in business

- Having a nervous breakdown

- Being defeated for nomination to Congress

- Being rejected for Land Officer

- Being defeated for the Senate and Vice President

Then Abraham Lincoln was elected president and his staunch stand against slavery carried him through to defeat the opposition during the Civil War. There were many times when he could have given up—when he could have believed the failure label that followed him for years. Abraham once again became president of the United States.

We have no idea, we can't even fathom what God is doing behind the scenes—preparing us and working all things together for our benefit. We must not give up. We must not stop short of our goals, our destiny because of what our past may have been or what people, society, and culture may label us.

A KINGLY EXAMPLE

As mentioned previously, King David had an affair with a married woman. When she became pregnant, David made arrangements for her husband to be killed in battle. He, rightfully so, was labeled an adulterer, a schemer, and a murderer. He also became a grieving father of the son who died because of his sin. David cried out to God for forgiveness. He took responsibility for his sin and asked that God would create in him a clean heart.

> *Create in me a clean heart, O God. Renew a loyal* [steadfast] *spirit within me* (Psalm 51:10).

Throughout the years, God had raised up David to lead His people and restore the land. David knew his place in the Lord's plan for his life and didn't give up—ultimately becoming the key in the lineage of Jesus the Messiah (Matthew 1:1; Acts 13:23; Revelation 22:16).

> *But now your* [Saul's] *kingdom must end, for the*
> *Lord has sought out a man after his own heart.*
> *The Lord has already appointed him* [David] *to*
> *be the leader of his people, because you have not*
> *kept the Lord's command* (1 Samuel 13:14).

David shed the negative labels in the past and earned the positive labels of a man after God's own heart as well as lover of the Lord, king of God's people, faithful friend, victorious warrior, compassionate ruler, and writer of most of the Psalms, which have brought hope and comfort to millions who have read them.

THE ULTIMATE EXAMPLE

Job, a God-fearing and obedient man, was targeted by satan who stripped him of his children and his wealth. We can learn many life lessons from Job and his refusal to allow any false labels to stick to him. During his satan-induced tragedies, Job was tormented even by his wife and friends who labeled him a loser, a failure, someone unworthy of God's favor. Yet Job declared:

> *"I came naked from my mother's womb, and I*
> *will be naked when I leave. The Lord gave me*
> *what I had, and the Lord has taken it away.*
> *Praise the name of the Lord!"* In all of this, Job
> *did not sin by blaming God* (Job 1:21-22).

Job's example of devotion to God has labeled him for centuries as a man of patience and endurance. He is a good example for people living in both biblical times and current times. His example of not sinning by blaming God is so vital for us to emulate today. We must take responsibility for ourselves—and we must pray for others. Job prayed—and his fortune and family were restored to him by God—in fact, he received double what he lost.

> *When Job prayed for his friends, the Lord restored his fortunes. In fact, the Lord gave him twice as much as before!* (Job 42:10)

I encourage you to start praying for your friends—and your enemies. If you want to see healing in your own life and see healing in your finances, start praying for other people's finances. Pray for another person's health. Start putting other people's needs before the Lord and you will see a major difference in your own life as well. As you give, you will receive: *"Your gift will return to you in full—pressed down, shaken together to make room for more, running over, and poured into your lap. The amount you give will determine the amount you get back"* (Luke 6:38).

Job didn't focus on his losses, he didn't focus on himself, he didn't label himself a victim, a loser, an orphan. No. He never gave up his faith in his heavenly Father. And the Bible says, *"Job lived 140 years after that, living to see four generations of his children and grandchildren. Then he died, an old man who had lived a long, full life"* (Job 42:16-17).

When you believe the labels God has assigned to you—loved, talented, worthy, valuable, a winner—you will make a positive difference in all that you do and all the people you meet. You will be known as the one who is always smiling, always has a kind word, always does every job to the best of your ability, and always offers a sincere prayer for people in need.

As Christians, we can't afford to act as if we have a sign hanging around our necks or a label on our foreheads stating, "Out of Order." The key to a *long, full life* of double blessings is to share our faith in our Savior with others—at every opportunity God sets before us.

PETER'S EXAMPLE

Jesus' disciple Peter is known for walking on water:

> *Then Peter called to him, "Lord, if it's really you, tell me to come to you, walking on the water." "Yes, come," Jesus said. So **Peter went over the side of the boat and walked on the water toward Jesus. But when he saw the strong wind and the waves, he was terrified and began to sink.** "Save me, Lord!" he shouted. **Jesus immediately reached out and grabbed him**. "You have so little faith," Jesus said. "Why did you doubt me?" When they climbed back into the boat, the wind stopped. Then the disciples worshiped him. "You really are the Son of God!" they exclaimed* (Matthew 14:28-33).

Peter is also known for panicking and falling into the water. When the wind and waves took his focus off Jesus, he was no longer walking supernaturally—he was sinking into the worldly waves of trouble.

When we get out of the boat with our focus on Jesus, we can supernaturally walk through whatever circumstances the world lays in front of us. Fear comes into our minds to kill, steal, and destroy our faith. Fear comes into our spirits to take our eyes off Jesus and redirect us toward difficulties and problems. Peter was afraid. When he cried out, *"Save me, Lord!"* immediately Jesus stretched out His hand and caught him from being overwhelmed by the wind and waves. We can always count on Jesus to respond *immediately* when we are afraid.

When Peter got out of the boat and out of his comfort zone, he may have thought, Wow, I'm standing on water! But this is impossible. How can this be happening? I can't really walk on water. I can't…it's impossible.

When we look at the impossible and concentrate on natural facts, we will begin to sink too. We must get our eyes off of the circumstances, off of the rough waters, off of the wind, off of what our finances are, off what financial institutions say, and off of the labels.

We have to focus our eyes on Jesus! When we concentrate on Jesus, we will see Him working incredibly good things in our lives. He will reach out, grab us, and bring us up to the top so we can walk on top of any circumstance we face. Then, like Peter and the other disciples, we will worship Him as the Son of God.

I encourage you to remove any labels that are not of God and stand proud but humble to be labeled a Christian. Never be ashamed of being labeled a Christian. Today in many areas of the world, that label is being perverted to mean something that it isn't. Stand up and stand strong for your faith—God will back you up, all the way.

PRAYER FOR REMOVING FALSE LABELS

As you read the following prayer, place your hand on your heart and believe that your prayer, like David's, will create in you a clean heart and a steadfast spirit.

> *Heavenly Father, I pray that You will remove all the labels that have been attached to me over the years that are not from You. Remove the false labels that may have been given to me by my parents, teachers, friends, family, employers, coworkers, neighbors, and other people who did not have my well-being in mind.*
>
> *Lord, I have held on too long to the negative comments people have said such as, "You'll never accomplish anything worthwhile. You can't be good at anything. You aren't smart enough to succeed," etc. God, please give me Your wisdom and Your favor to become what You want me to be. Help me to be strong and to never give up living for You.*
>
> *God, right now in the name of Jesus, remove the label of being broke, the label of never having*

enough. Lord, remove the label of always being tired; give me energy to move forward. Remove the labels of being stupid, clumsy, unattractive. Remove the death sentence of the medical report, in Jesus' name. Lord God, remove the labels that the wind and the waves of the world have attached to me so I can concentrate on Jesus and on Your will and ways for me to live free.

God, I am your child. I am victorious, healthy, wealthy, wise, strong, and loving. I am a witness to Your love and peace. I want to walk in Your ways. Thank You, Father, for the plans You have for my life and my destiny. I am blessed! Hallelujah!

Chapter 4

FOCUS

God gave me a word—FOCUS. Chapter 3 mentioned "focus" throughout, and it's the title of this chapter. You can chart your course in life, but if you don't focus on the compass of God's direction, you're not going to reach your destination. You must be able to focus.

After brainstorming the word "focus," although not confined to these, the following are a few words I came up with to define the word using each letter—FOCUS:

F

- **Faith**

- **Fun**

- **Forward**—March forward.

- **Fruitful**

- **Finances**—You can't fulfill your God-given destiny if you are strapped financially and in debt. To fulfill your dreams, you have to be financially solvent. God's heart is giving, and you are binding God's hands until you release your own hand.

The F you *don't* want is "Forget—forgetting your calling." If you have the call of God on your life and say, "Forget it, I'm not focusing on my call," you won't live an abundant life. But also know that even if you try to forget it, the call is still within you. It's up to you to embrace it.

O

- **Overcome**—Be an overcomer.

- **Outlook**—You need a good outlook on life.

- **Optimist**—See the positive in everything.

I am an ultra-mega-phenomenal-off-the-chart-irritatingly-optimistic person—ask anybody. I have incredible dreams and visions, and it takes finances to bring them into reality. For example, Joan Hunter Ministries is claiming the land near our headquarters for God. We don't want the wrong things coming into close proximity. We need funds to buy and build on that land, so nothing comes in that isn't of God.

C

- **Circumstance**s—You can focus on your circumstances—or focus on Jesus.

- **Clarity**—Clarity in your vision.

- **Creativity**—*Oh, I'm not creative at all,* you may think. But you *do* have an imagination. I've heard people say that imagination is of the devil. No! Imagination is from God. But He *does* say to cast down all vain imaginations, which includes lust and other worthless thoughts.

U

- **Understanding**

- **Unique**—You are unique.

My mom had cataract surgery and afterward she didn't need to wear her glasses. I was excited one day when I found her glasses and put them on. Then it hit me, "Because I'm Frances Hunter's daughter, how often have people tried to put Mom on me? And attempted to put God's call for Mom onto me?"

When Mom was around eighty years of age, people came up to me and said, "Your mom is getting older. Do you know your mom's ministry?" Meaning I was to eventually step into my mother's shoes. At the time, I was *not* going to be put in a Frances Hunter box, so I went into the next service and did everything opposite of the way my mom did. Praise God, I'm free of that rebellion now.

Many years ago, one of my parents became sick before a meeting in Rehoboth, Massachusetts, and said, "Joan, you're going on alone."

"What? Me, alone? There are five hundred people waiting to hear you…and you're sending me? Someone they've never heard of?"

I was apprehensive, but I went. The first night I said, "If you've come to hear from Charles or Frances Hunter, you're going to be disappointed—but if you've come to hear from God, you won't be." I did the service the way I'd been trained and how I'd seen Mom and Dad do it. That night I went back to my hotel room feeling good about the evening. I said, "Father God, I thank You for an awesome meeting."

"You did a really good job," God responded. "Tomorrow, how about you do it My way instead of your mom and dad's way."

The thing is, I can't wear my mom's calling. I have her mantle, my dad's, a little bit of Kathryn Kuhlman's, Amy Semple McPherson's, and others. But I must follow my own calling from God. Mom's glasses won't work for me. But my little readers help me read fine print. Oftentimes we emulate those we've been around rather than being our own unique selves.

This point was brought home to me the other day in a sweet way. I have an earpiece for my phone. When it rings, it tells me who is calling. I can then choose to answer by saying, "Answer." My young granddaughter has a fake phone and she now walks around saying, "Answer! Answer!" She's emulating what she's heard, which at her age is adorable. But it's not cute if I'm in the pulpit and simply repeating the teaching words of Kenneth Hagin or Frances Hunter.

I was recently at a meeting where a lady just preached her dad's sermons—and he had died forty years prior. Her book table offered only his work to purchase. This isn't good. Each of us have to receive fresh revelation from God and walk in what God's calls us individually to do.

I have no problem with people who want to be like me, not copying me, but following my mold and model in the area of healing. If you start teaching on healing, you'll begin to see supernatural manifestations of healing wherever you go. You don't have to follow me verbatim, but it will give you boundaries and basic guidelines.

For example, one day at the pulpit, I said, "Excuse me, folks." I continued, "Answer. Hello. I'm in a service. May I call you later? You need me to pray with you right now? May I have one of my prayer teams call you? No, you just want me? Well, I'm kind of busy. Give me about another hour and I'll call you back. I know you're disappointed, but I promise, I'll call you back. Okay, thanks."

I knew some in the audience were thinking, *She took a call? In the middle of the service?* Many thought the call was a fake. That was true, it wasn't an authentic phone call. I don't answer phone calls during a service, but I often do receive calls asking me to pray. When preaching or teaching, I must remain focused on teaching and not be distracted by the phone so that people will receive God's message through me.

What's the number-one cause of accidents today? Texting. Not drugs, not alcohol, but texting. Distractions. If you concentrate on what's in your rearview mirror, you're going to run into what's right in front of you.

As Christians, if you concentrate on your past and believe that God can't use you because of it, then guess what? You're going to end up on a dead-end street. Please understand that your past is under Christ's shed blood and you are now as white as snow. If you sin later today or next week, repent! Quickly. Don't keep sinning and sinning and then keep repenting and repenting—that's not true repentance. Repentance means that once you sin, you repent, and you don't repeat it again.

Some people believe that once you've repented in salvation, that's it—but that's not what is written in the Bible! What's under the blood is under the blood; yet occasionally, we need an additional dousing of blood.

Back to **U** in **FOCUS**:

- **Underlying**—Identify the bad and get rid of it. For example, anger can be an

underlying negative influence that needs
to be dealt with. Also, Unforgiveness.

U also stands for You—Someone said that her doctor
told her, "Quit taking care of everybody else. Think about
yourself for a change." I understand that comment because
I want to take care of my family. When I wrote this message, there were six extra people living in my house, four of
which were grandchildren who adore me. As I ran around
the house one morning getting ready to go out, I thought,
I need to stay focused! After responding to numerous requests
for attention, I finally had to say, "Grandma's got to go!" I
was having fun, but I still needed to stay focused.

It's so hard to spend time on yourself, especially if you're
a mom. It was months after Charity was born before I even
took a shower. If you're a mom, you probably laughed reading that because you understand. I thought, *I can't leave the
baby in bed while I take a shower and my husband's at work.
What if something happened while I'm in there?* I finally snuck
one in. It was hard figuring out when to do something for
me because I was so focused on the baby, who needed me
twenty-four hours a day. Praise God she's almost forty now.

But we *do* have to think about ourselves sometimes. I'm
not talking about being egotistical. What I mean is, we need
to get enough rest, food, relaxation, and spend fun time
with our family.

I spent a week in California with fourteen out of sixteen of our family. I didn't feel I could take time off, yet I
made it a priority to go. And God supernaturally provided
the way. I had three to five grandkids sleeping in my room

every night—but we had a blast. That's a lot of excitement for a week. And then I came home and slept.

While in California, my two-year-old grandson rode on a little merry-go-round in a fish that looked like Elmo. The other day he called me and said, "Elmo fish, Elmo fish." I didn't think he'd remember that ride for more than a few days, but it's forever ingrained into his mind because I, Grandma, took time out to spend a week with him.

S

- **Start. Start. Start. Start**—Even though S is the last letter of FOCUS, you must *start*. Start focusing on Jesus; start focusing on your calling; start putting your dreams into action steps; start....

- **Strategies**—Sixteen years ago in March, my divorce was finalized. Two days later I had my annual checkup. After a mammogram, I had to have a sonogram. They found cancer in my body. I had already lost my finances and our church because of sin in our house. And now at this point, I realized I was losing my life. Devastated, I was not having a good day.

While lying on the examining table, focusing on the sonogram, which I was able to watch, I thought, *Put some flowers in my hand and I'll look like I'm in a casket.* Then I thought, I need to find an outfit to wear, and I'd better plan everything out because my children have been through enough. I don't want them worrying about anything where my death and burial is concerned.

But suddenly it hit me—*I have four reasons to live: Charity, Spice, Melody, and Abigail—my girls.* And I literally began slapping my face, saying out loud, "No, I'm *not* going to die. I'm going to live and declare the works of the Lord. My girls need me. They'll need me to help them with their wedding dresses. That's the mother's role, and I don't want anybody else taking my place. I'm going to have fun shopping for a wedding dress and helping pay for each daughter's wedding!"

At the time of writing this book, three daughters are married, praise God, and we had enough money for nice weddings. Glory to God! The fourth daughter's husband is going to be the most awesome, incredible man we've ever met in this entire world. They will be perfect for each other.

Note: The word "cancer" should start with an n for nail in your coffin. Too often this dreaded disease is known as the "Big C." Well, I consider cancer as a little c—Christ is the "BIG C!" Hallelujah!

By now you know that you have to focus. The definition in the dictionary for FOCUS is three pages long. Focus can be a noun or an adverb, meaning emphasis, accent, priority, attention, and concentration. Often an organization's mission statement emphasizes focusing on helping people. Having a personal mission statement causes you to focus on your goal.

FOCUSED PRAYER

I make sure there are focused prayers in my books. I know that if I lay hands on somebody and say, "In Jesus' name, be healed," God can heal you. I know that works. But I prefer to pray for a specific outcome, a particular issue.

For example, in the natural, if I need surgery for a certain ailment, I certainly don't want a generic operation. And I surely don't want a doctor who is performing laser treatment or radiation on me to say, "The problem is somewhere around here, Joan. I don't know quite where...so we'll just cover the whole area." No! The treatment should focus on the exact spot.

In the spiritual, the prayer should focus on the specific issue as well. By focusing my prayers, I see about 97 percent of the people I pray for healed. Instantly. I'm going for 100 percent this year!

We had a service in Eastern Pennsylvania, and a woman there was a wreck. She was diagnosed with bipolar and schizophrenia disorders and other ailments. She left that meeting whole, healed. But the interesting thing, she handed me a list of her ailments and said, "Please don't say any of these words when you pray for me."

"Okay," I said.

"I mean it. Don't say anything on this list," and she backs up about five feet.

"Okay. I can pray directly, yet indirectly without using schizophrenia and bipolar and so forth, and we can focus on what the real problem is."

A short time later, I heard from the woman. She said, "My life is totally changed because of that moment you prayed for me." Hallelujah! Focused prayers went right for the trauma and got rid of it. Isn't God amazing!?

When writing, if you want the reader to focus on a word or phrase, you highlight or italicize or bold it. Or if I need something transcribed and corrected, I circle it and say what I want done, drawing attention to that particular portion of the text.

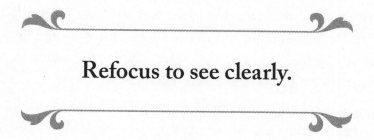

Refocus to see clearly.

When choosing a photograph, for instance, if the image is not in focus, it's deleted. Likewise, if you're focused, but your vision gets out of alignment or becomes blurry, you can't go any further in your pursuit. Consider this: if you develop a cataract and can't see clearly, you don't say, "Well, I guess I'm going to be blind the rest of my life." No! The first thing you do is pray. Number two, you have cataract surgery to remove the problem. Then you can focus again.

Whatever is blocking your vision or keeping you from seeing clearly needs to be removed surgically through the spirit realm so you can focus on all that God has for you.

We all need to refocus at times. When you walk outside on a sunny day, what happens? Your eyes refocus or adjust to the light. When you receive a promotion at work or accept a ministry position, you have to refocus on the new circumstances and adjust how you see your future. If God calls you to the prophetic and/or healing ministry, you not only have the anointing for healing, you also have the knowledge, which is like nitroglycerin—making life explosive, because you have the knowledge to appropriate the power of God.

When giving birth by the Lamaze method, the mother is told, "Focus, focus. You won't feel the pain." I had four girls by natural childbirth. I did a lot of focusing and heavy breathing because my labors were long—but I didn't need any pain medication because I was focused.

In every area of our lives, from childbirth through adulthood, we must choose to focus on our goals. We have to fine-tune the call of God in our lives and in our mission statement. When we understand this, life becomes clearer.

FOCUSED VISION

God has given us vision. He's also given us peripheral vision. No doubt you have heard that moms have eyes in the back of their head. Of course, that's not really true, but it often seems that way.

I actually have phenomenal natural vision and can see things most people don't notice. I also have spiritual vision, which means I can see disease, sickness, and heartache. This vision is part of my God-given calling that I use to further His Kingdom.

The vision statement of Joan Hunter Ministries is to equip believers to take the healing power of God beyond the four walls of the church, to the four corners of the earth. The four corners are your family, your neighborhood, where you shop, and where you work. If you're not faithful in those four areas, don't expect to go to Hawaii or the Ukraine to minister on a missions trip. You have to take care of your own community and circle of influence that God has given you. If you don't care about those, why would God send you around the world?

However, our first focus must be on healing our own body, mind, soul, spirit, and finances. We need to be whole and healthy so we can minister health and wellness to others. Our peripheral vision is to teach us how to be better people. Peripheral vision *also includes* teaching on the prophetic, which is in the area of equipping.

The most important thing is, we must remain focused on what God has called us to do. There are some people who seem to be able to do everything, but even they need to stop and say, "God, what do You want me to do?" And as you begin to focus on His vision for you, you will see that particular area develop and improve.

I'm going to share a couple of other things along those lines. In the physical realm, if you have trouble seeing in the distance, that means you're nearsighted and you can be fitted for glasses with the correct prescription to correct the problem. In the spirit realm, there are a lot of things God has called you to do, yet you may not see them clearly.

We all are given knowledge on a need-to-know basis. If God told me, right now, everything I'm going to do this coming year, I'd probably pass out at the enormity of it all. So, God reveals a little at a time as we need to plan, then gives us clarity for that direction so we can become focused.

Have you ever opened a closet door and thought, "I need to clean out this messy closet"? But then the phone rings. Then somebody needs you in the kitchen. Soon you realize you need to fix the evening meal. Suddenly, it's the end of the day and that closet is still a mess. Or you haven't yet written that chapter for your book. There are so many distractions that keep you from doing what you were born to do. Therefore, you must choose to intentionally set aside time to focus on your vision from God.

YOUR YEAR OF RECOVERY

I received a message from Pastor Patricia King saying, "Put your seatbelts on for what's getting ready to happen. There is a shift happening."

The shift is here, but we have to focus on what lies ahead. We must learn not to be distracted from what God wants us to focus on. Debt and lack can be huge distractions, but don't let anyone or anything take your focus off God. Today is the time to believe Jehovah Jireh, who will supply all of our needs.

In November, somebody gave very sacrificially and it's phenomenal how God has supernaturally manifested that offering in every area of that person's life. All their financial situations have been handled as a result.

Can you imagine how Abraham felt when asked to sacrifice his son, the child of promise? And how his heart rejoiced when God provided the lamb instead? (See Genesis 22.) God may ask you to sacrifice something you love dearly. Sometimes He asks just to see if you're willing to give it up—and then He provides a lamb.

I have no sons, only daughters; but I have grandsons. And I don't think I could sacrifice any of them. There were times when they were young when they exhausted me with their constant activity and tried my patience—but praise God, I learned early about putting them on the altar.

The New King James Version of the Bible says in First Samuel 30:18-19:

> *David recovered all that the Amalekites had carried away, and David rescued his two wives. And nothing of theirs was lacking, either small or great, sons or daughters, spoil or anything which they had taken from them;* **David recovered all.**

David recovered most of what he'd lost. No! Wait a minute. The Bible says *David recovered all*. The legal term "all" means including everything, excluding nothing. David got everything back.

Like David, this is our year to recover all! We're shifting into a year of recovery, into all that God has promised us. This is our year to see all the dreams and visions that He's given us come to fruition. We're going to see an incredible, supernatural move of God like we've never seen before.

I don't know about you, but I'm not going to just watch from the sideline. I'm focused on being a participant, a primary player, on the first string, part of the A team. I'm a woman on the front lines. Hallelujah!

There's a time to be passive and there's a time to fight. If you want to see me fight, say something bad about my children or grandchildren. Obviously, there is nothing bad to say, but if you could think of something, you would see another whole side of me come out ready to defend them.

I'm not the same person as I was seventeen years ago. I used to be the lamest, weakest person you could ever fathom, with no self-esteem. About the age of seven, I was diagnosed with a learning disability and told I would never be able to read or write or ever accomplish anything other than wash dishes for a living. I spent twenty-some years of my life focusing on what I couldn't do.

With four daughters and many grandchildren, I definitely have washed a lot of dishes. I've never been paid for that chore—except for all the benefits of being a mother and grandmother. And praise God for paper plates, too! But the thing is, I believed what I was told and focused on that—and I didn't do a thing to change the scenario others painted for me.

If I had had a choice of career, I would have been a nurse or a doctor. How ironic is that? Today I am a healer for God, and my career is a whole lot easier with a lot less blood, because the blood of Christ the Messiah has already been shed! To become the person God created me to be, I had to shed those false labels and focus on my goal to help people and see them healed—and that's exactly what I did and continue to do.

PRE-BORN TRAUMA PRAYER FOCUS

I want to tell you a story, but let me begin by being clear on this major point. Charles Hunter was my dad—he adopted me. My brother's father had died, and my parents separated the week of their wedding. One day when my mom was around five months pregnant with me, my natural father, whom God used only to bring me into this world, came back to kill my mom, my brother, and me.

When you pray to be healed from trauma, go back to conception, because you don't know what really went on while you were inside your mother's womb. A few years ago, God gave me the revelation that the trauma of gunshots during my brain development while yet in my mother's uterus is what caused my disability. But praise the Lord, He broke the generational curses of murder and anger!

One lady told me that when she was in her mother's womb, her dad shot her mom. When she pretended to be dead, he shot and killed himself. Mom and child survived, but the child had a learning disability until I prayed for her and God removed that trauma. Now she's excelling.

When I was seven, I wish I had known that prayer was all I needed. Because there was no trauma while my children or grandchildren were in the womb, none of my children or grandchildren have any learning disabilities. I'm not a brilliant person today in the natural, I know my limitations, yet I'm an anointed person. If you give me an 800-page agreement, I won't have a clue what it says. But I'm smart enough to take it to someone and say, "Would you please read this, explain it, and make sure all the details are correct?" We all need help from time to time. Don't be too proud to ask for it.

In a few months, I'll have a total of seventeen books published. I know by now that I must stay focused on each book, otherwise I wouldn't have finished writing even the first one. My books are intentionally written on a ninth-grade reading level and with the KISS method— Keep it Simple, Saints—so that everyone can understand how to prophesy, how to pray for the sick, and how to deal with trauma.

When seeking God's wisdom for your life and learning what I hope to teach you in my books, you will quickly earn a PhD degree. *A PhD?* you may wonder. Yes! A PhD in **P**reaching, **H**ealing, and **D**eliverance. God has given you a calling—with His leading, you can preach, heal, and deliver people from their bondage. God has given you dreams so you can walk them out, achieve each one, and then dream even bigger. You may not be dreaming large enough. Let's look at Moses again.

MOSES

Exodus 14 tells us that Moses led all of God's people away from Egypt toward the Red Sea where they faced crossing a wide, deep river or be killed. I can imagine the conversations among the crowd, "We're never going to make it!" "We're going to drown!" "Oh my God, what are we going to do?" The people were doubting, they were focused only on the natural, the seemingly impossible circumstances facing them.

What was Moses' reaction? Did he focus on the sea? Or did he focus on God? Moses didn't whine, whimper, or pull out his hair. Instead, he focused on God, held out his rod, and whoosh, the sea opened and a path for the Israelites appeared. They walked across on dry land. Moses had developed an intimate relationship with God. He learned God's ways and was even privileged to speak with God face to face. He was a friend of God.

I am a friend of God too; in fact, I'm His favorite. You are too. Each of us is His favorite, and that's all that matters. He loves us individually as His special child. When we focus on God, He focuses on us.

Moses was focused on God. He was introduced to Yahweh at the burning bush (Exodus 3:1-6). The Angel of the Lord manifested Himself to a human. Moses also knew Him through the pillar of cloud by day and the pillar of fire by night (Exodus 13:21-22). God even told Moses to speak to a rock to receive water for the thirsty masses of people and animals. Moses had to feed a million people. Did he panic? No. Moses prayed and God sent down manna from Heaven for the Israelites to gather and eat.

ABANDONING COMFORT ZONES

These supernatural manifestations demonstrate the powerful presence of God being visible to humans in a tangible, observable form. God has given us dreams to walk out, making them realities. A shift in the ordinary is getting ready to happen—life and things are going to change. We're way past first, second, third, and fourth gear. Yet life will only change when you become more committed or more focused on your dreams and the call on your life. God wants you to get out of your comfort zone, to get out of the boat like Peter did.

In our ministry services, it's normal protocol for someone to introduce the speaker. Melody, my daughter, normally introduces me, but one time she was teaching, so I asked a young man who works with the ministry to introduce me.

His eyes got so big! He has served faithfully for years and doesn't miss a service—even sleeps in the building sometimes because he lives so far away. When faithfully serving a ministry like ours, there is a possibility of being called to the microphone or serving in a variety of capacities. But for this young man to actually introduce me was pushing him out of his comfort zone and asking him to "walk on water." He hesitated for a second, agreed, came up on the platform, and took his rightful place of authority. He knew, beyond a shadow of a doubt, that he could do it. But there's a difference between *knowing* you can do it and actually *doing* it. I'm happy to say that he did a great job. Later he said, "Thank you for making me do that."

We all have things that appear to be barriers of water that we can't walk through or walk upon. But there comes a time when we need to get out of the boat, get out of our comfort zones, and stop saying, "But it's just so nice here, I want to stay put." No, now is the time to walk forth toward and with Jesus.

DISTRACTIONS

God blessed me with a house on a lake. My daughter, her husband, and four children moved in with me. The children are now in public school, but they used to be homeschooled. When working on their schoolwork, they would stop and look out the window and say, "Look at the baby ducks!" Or the neighborhood cat would come look in the window at them and they would stop studying and make faces. It was difficult to get them to concentrate on their school-work because there was such fun, beautiful distractions just beyond the window.

Interruptions will happen. We all fall into a ditch or a pothole while journeying down the road of life. In fact, I was pushed into a ditch about sixteen years ago. Not physically, but spiritually and emotionally. I could either stay down or get up. *"Yea, though I walk through the valley of the shadow of death..."* (Psalm 23:4 KJV). Just remember it's *walk through* not *live in*. When you hit a rough patch in the road, regroup, refocus, and keep going. When something horrible happens to you, don't concentrate on it. Get your focus off of the pain and focus only on the Healer. As long as Peter kept his eyes on Jesus, he could walk on the water. But when he got distracted, suddenly, he began to sink.

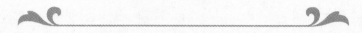

Troubles are to walk through, not to live in.

I don't want you to begin to sink, much less sink and drown. I love the song "Oceans" by Hillsong United. A portion of the lyrics encourage us:

> *Your grace abounds in deepest waters,*
>
> *Your sovereign hand will be my guide.*
>
> *Where feet may fail and fear surround me,*
>
> *You've never failed and You won't start now.*
>
> *So I will call upon Your name,*
>
> *And keep my eyes above the waves.*
>
> *When oceans rise,*
>
> *My soul will rest in Your embrace;*
>
> *For I am Yours and You are mine.*
>
> *Spirit lead me where my trust is*
> *without borders,*

Let me walk upon the waters,

Wherever You would call me.

Take me deeper than my feet could ever wander

And my faith will be made stronger

In the presence of my Saviour.

God has called you to do more than you have done so far—getting out of your comfort zone is essential if you are to accomplish His will for you. God has called me to do a whole lot more than I'm doing already. I don't know how I'm going to fit it in, but God's knows. And I know that my horizons are expanding, even on a daily basis. I am so excited about what God is and will be doing in my life.

God can fine-tune His call on our lives. And our peripheral vision needs to come into alignment, not become a distraction. Get rid of as many interruptions as possible. The Word says in James 4:8, *"Come close to God, and God will come close to you...."* As you become focused on God and God's heart, you will see every area of your life come into complete alignment, as you have hoped and prayed.

This is the year of turning our "hopes" into "haves." We're going to have an incredible, anointed, healing ministry in every area.

I'm going to pray over you and believe that God will remove any demonic cataracts and any blurred vision will be restored to clear focus. I encourage you to examine yourself. What are you really focusing on?

PRAYER FOR FOCUS

Father, right now, I thank You. I thank You that this is a time of coming into focus, refocusing, fine-tuning, getting rid of distractions, and any form of compromise that can be blinding and deceptive. Father, in the name of Jesus, I speak clarity of vision. Father, in the name of Jesus, I thank You that Your power is going through my words, permeating into this reader's heart and removing any demonic cataracts, any lack of vision. Father, fine-tune this person's lenses. Provide Holy Spirit glasses made just for this friend to see You and the call You have on this precious life. Make it clearer than ever before.

Father, as always, I speak an impartation of anointing in the area of healing, but also in the area of finances—for greater breakthrough. I pray that the seeds that this person has sown will be supernaturally multiplied—so quickly that not even a day goes by with anything missing in the bank. Father, I thank You for giving this reader the funds to fuel every dream and help finance all that You've called him or her to do.

And, Father, I speak wisdom into this person, in Jesus' name. I speak dreams and visions like never experienced before. I pray that this person receives better than 20/20 vision for focus on You. I speak to any kind of brain fog to be removed, in Jesus' name. Any demonic distractions to go and not return, in Jesus' name. I speak life, health, wholeness, and fruition of what You have called this dear reader to do, in Jesus' name. Amen.

Chapter 5

TIME TO STEP OUT

*I*t's time!

Isaiah 40:31 (NKJV) says, *"But those who wait on the Lord shall renew their strength; they shall mount up with wings like eagles, they shall run and not be weary, they shall walk and not faint."*

"Wait on the Lord"—what does that mean? Oftentimes people misconstrue what waiting on the Lord actually means. For instance, one day I saw a guy sitting in a chair and rocking. He said, "I'm just waiting on God."

"You know what?" I said, "You're rocking in the wrong place." He had rocked so long and so hard that he actually broke the chair—just waiting to hear from God.

I've heard people say, "I'm waiting for God to call me, waiting for the call on my life." I say, don't wait anymore—the longer you wait, the more you postpone the call on your life. God wants you to walk out your destiny and take those first steps today.

I don't think anybody else can do what I do as well as I do. That's not ego, it's fact. I can say that because God has called me to do what I'm doing. He's anointed me. And God brought people alongside to help me because I don't have to do it alone, we do it as a team.

Jesus had a team—twelve guys. Jesus changed the world and His disciples were along for the ride—for all the ups and downs of life on earth. I need more people than He did to help me with my calling. People who are committed to living out their calling as they work as a team with me.

What is more important than fulfilling your destiny, God's call on your life? Nothing is more important—it's why you were born. There are many "life coaches" right now who claim to be able to direct people toward their destiny. Some people consider these coaches a necessity because they don't have any idea where to go or what to do in life. They need someone else to encourage them verbally or give them a swift kick to get them started. But what they really need is to listen to and obey the Holy Spirit within themselves to show them the Way, the Truth, and the Life.

GPS—GOD'S POSITIONING SYSTEM

However, we do need encouragement to follow through with what God has called us to do. We need trustworthy, godly people around us who will tell us if we start heading in the wrong direction. Likewise, I encourage you to become a mentor to someone who is searching for meaning. I love mentoring people in the Kingdom of God and seeing them launch out into full-time ministry to become all that God has meant them to be! It's a win for that person and a win for me as well. You too!

Let me ask you, "Why not now?" Now is a good time to begin! Today is a very important day on the calendar because it's now and you're not going to wait anymore. You can jump into serving Him—no longer waiting on the sidelines.

The verse at the beginning of this chapter says those who wait—but it also says, *"they mount up...they run... they walk...."* In other words, they *take action!* They don't wait indefinitely.

When I get to Heaven, I don't want God to say, "I had so much more for you, but you waited too long. You were a chicken. You were afraid to step out. You liked your comfort zone too much, staying home instead of traveling. And you didn't like spending the time to write."

This chapter is about encouraging you, stimulating you to pray about your next step in life. God has so much more for you. I hate wasted anointing. I hate wasted energy. I hate it when I see people a year later and nothing has changed. They have taken no action to improve or advance their careers, financial status, relationships, etc. And yet they wonder why they are still in the same rut. Be willing to change.

Be willing to change— climb out of the rut.

An unknown author wrote, "If nothing ever changed, there'd be no butterflies." I agree. And like caterpillars, we need to transform into all that God has for us and fly higher, see more and do more. God is positioning you to do great things for Him—for yourself. God is positioning you to move in His will for your life, taking you toward fulfilling your prophetic vision.

God, in His infinite wisdom created all creatures great and small. From grand elephants to tiny caterpillars that turn into beautiful butterflies. Chicks emerge from eggs at just the right time. If you crack and open a fertilized egg before it's time to hatch—it will die. It must come out of the shell on its own at the correct time.

I'm trying my best to encourage you to come out of your shell. But I can't do it for you. You have to peck at the shell from the inside until you're free. Once you break through, you will not regret it—you'll have exciting and life-changing experiences that you will never forget.

The chick inside the egg says, "Hey, it's getting crowded and uncomfortable in here." So, it works on getting out.

Tap, tap, tap. In the meantime, the chick's beak, wings, feet, and body becomes stronger, preparing it to live in the world outside the shell. And because of that time of preparation, when the chick emerges, it can walk, fly, and eat—take care of itself.

I think you've been preparing long enough. It's time to get out of your shell and do what God has called you to do.

EXPECT AN ANSWER

One of my favorite handy tools is WD-40. If something squeaks or sticks, I put a little WD-40 on it and it's good as new. I'm very glad the inventor didn't stop at WD-39! Persistence is key to success.

As mentioned earlier, a wall-hanging in my house says, "Never give up. Go under, go over, go through, but never give up." That statement is there because about seventeen years ago, my life was destroyed and I could have easily quit—quit ministry, quit everything. It would have been so easy. But I decided not to give up. And I want to encourage you to never, never give up on the life you are meant to live.

James 1:6-8 says:

> ***When you ask him*** [God], *be sure that your faith is in God alone. **Do not waver,** for a person with divided loyalty is as unsettled as a wave of the sea that is blown and tossed by the wind. **Such people should not expect to receive** anything from the Lord. Their loyalty is divided*

between God and the world, and they are unstable in everything they do.

The Living Bible says it this way:

> **When you ask him [God], be sure that you really expect him to tell you**, *for a doubtful mind will be as unsettled as a wave of the sea that is driven and tossed by the wind; and every decision you then make will be uncertain, as you turn first this way and then that.* **If you don't ask with faith, don't expect the Lord to give you any solid answer** (James 1:6-8 TLB).

Have you heard doubtful-minded people ask:

- "Has God called me to the ministry?"

- "Did God really call me to the ministry?"

- "I don't remember God calling me, did He call?"

Do you want to be doubtful, double-minded, unsettled, wavering back and forth, not sure whether God has called you into the ministry? Well, let me answer that for you—no, you don't want to be confused. And yes! He *has* called you into the ministry!

Has God called you into a full-time traveling ministry? Well, He doesn't call everyone to travel. But yes, He may have; and if that's what God has called you to do, then get focused and hang on for a fun ride. Get into what God has for you to do and launch out. If He calls you to write a book, write one. If He calls you to minister to your neighborhood, go. The point is, don't put off whatever you feel God has called you to do.

Consider this—how many people have not been reached with the Good News because you haven't written your book? How many people have not been reached because you're not blogging on the Internet or commenting on Facebook? You can minister around the world through Facebook. You can minister around the world by tweeting on your phone.

It's time, it's time, it's time—now is your time!

SET YOUR CLOCK

I have a friend who sets her alarm to go off at 8 o'clock in the morning—and every five minutes for the next hour—before she gets up. You really don't want to share a room with her. Ring, snooze, ring, snooze, every five minutes. The first time this happened when we shared a room, I said, "Are you ever going to get up?"

"Yeah, I'm going to get up at nine."

"Then why did you set your alarm for 8, 8:05, 8:10, and every five minutes? I would have liked to have slept till nine."

My point is, how many times has God said to you, "Get up, get up, I've called you"?

You may hear Him, but you hit the snooze button and go back to your nice, warm comfort zone. You're actually hitting the snooze button on your calling. God doesn't want you to snooze away your life. He wants you to do what He's called you to do. He wants you to rise up and use the gifts and talents and wisdom He gave you.

But I don't know what to do, you may be thinking. Who do I ask? Who do I go to for wisdom? Who am I supposed to turn to?

Pray first. When you pray, people's names or faces will come to mind who are ready and willing to help point you in the right direction. For instance, if you want to know about healing—here I am, Joan Hunter, forty-five years in the healing ministry. I not only already have a wealth of information, but I learned even more this week—and will learn more next week. I enjoy an awesome, constant learning curve as I serve people around the world.

YOUR SPIRITUAL GIFT

God gives me revelations, and He doesn't want me to be quiet about them. It may sound strange, but I'm thrilled that God gives me revelation because He trusts me to share my revelations with people who need to hear from Him. And He trusts my writing abilities too, which allows my books to be published and change people's lives worldwide for His glory.

In First Corinthians 12, Paul says there are different kinds of spiritual gifts, but the same Holy Spirit as the

Source. Likewise, there are different kinds of service, but we serve the same Lord. God works in different ways in each of our lives, but He's the same God who does the work through us. Paul says in First Corinthians 12:7 that each one of us are given a spiritual gift to help the entire church: *"A spiritual gift is given to each of us so we can help each other."*

And as it says in the parable of the talents, if we use the gift we're given—we'll be given more (Matthew 25:14-30). You have the wisdom, knowledge, anointing, and the call to help change the world. Too many believers are sitting on their gift in the boat. It's time to step into your destiny.

MOVE ON

I'm sure you understand the power of words. Maybe you've said or heard someone say:

- "You'll never get over this."
- "You'll never get any better."
- "You'll never make it financially."
- "You're so stupid."
- "You'll never be able to learn, you'll never be able to write."
- "You only have about two years to live."

All this had been spoken over me. In 2000, because of cancer, I was given approximately two years to live. But praise the Lord! That was more than sixteen years ago and I'm still here—cancer-free—and serving God! God healed me in every area of my life—body, mind, soul, spirit, and finances. Glory be to God!

When you get down and start living in a rut—an open-ended grave—God is not going to just pull you out. He wants you to become determined enough to pull yourself out and depend on Him for the strength needed. We must be resolved to live and to do what God has called us to do.

We need to rid our minds of some of the old teachings and mindsets that women can't be used in the pulpit or allowed to have leadership positions in the church. It's a good thing Paul didn't think that way. Over and over again we read in his letters where he praises the various women leaders in the church. God wants to use all people, not just men.

A divorced lady came up to me one time and said, "Would you please pray for me?"

I said, "Okay, I'll pray. How long has he been out of your life?"

"Twenty-nine years."

"Okay," I said.

"He's remarried and has children with her."

With that comment, the compassion I felt for this woman went out the window and the prophet in me came out. "You need to move on," I said. "He's not coming back. And you don't want to bring death to his current marriage just to get him back."

She looked at me with tears in her eyes. "But..."

"You have to let go of the grief and the guilt," I said. "Let yourself receive the Lord's forgiveness and move on with your life. Your husband has stolen another twenty-nine years of your life. But now it's time to do what God has called you to do for Him."

Back in 2000, when I was divorced, everyone told me that I would feel better in seven or eight years. I thought, *I'll never get over this.* But I put my eyes on Jesus and said, "I am not going to give that man seven, five, or any more years of my life. I'm going to get over this and make sure everyone in the same situation knows that they can get over it too." And I got over it—I moved on. Hallelujah!

Sometime later, my oldest daughter said something that meant the world. She said, "I really admire you, Mom, because you don't hold anything against Dad. You never speak ill of him."

I realized then that Jesus had healed me all the way down to the cellular level of my body. You, too, can forget the hurtful past; and with His help, the pain and guilt simply go away. Isn't that awesome?

ONE MOMENT IN TIME

One moment in time can change your life, and perhaps reading this book will be a pivotal point in your life. Maybe you'll look back and see that everything changed at this moment. I pray that will happen for you.

A young salesman was ordained because he thought that's what he was supposed to do. The weekend following his ordination, as I was prophesying from the pulpit, my words triggered something in his heart. The young man went back home, started praying for people, and many were being healed.

Soon people began saying, "We really need a miracle center." So, the young man opened a miracle center. The next thing we knew, people said, "We don't have a place to worship, we need a church." The young, former salesman now pastors a church—all this happened within the last four years. His whole life changed in that one moment in time—the moment when he accepted God's calling on his life.

Mark 16:15-18 cites Jesus' Great Commission:

> *He said to them,* **"Go into all the world and preach the gospel** *to every creature. He who believes and is baptized will be saved; but he who does not believe will be condemned. And these signs will follow those who believe: In My name they will cast out demons; they will speak with new tongues; they will take up serpents; and if they drink anything deadly, it will by no means hurt them; they will lay hands on the sick, and they will recover"* (NKJV).

This means that you are going to lay hands on the sick and see them recover; cast out demons, the whole bit. This is what God has called His children to do. It's time!

Queen Esther had only one moment in time to save the Jewish people from slaughter. She spent a lot of time preparing physically, emotionally, and spiritually because she knew she would be putting her life on the line by approaching the king without being called. It would have been instant death if the king hadn't held out his scepter to her. But Esther kept her eyes on the one true God and did what He had called her to do. And she saved the whole nation.

God is raising you up for such a time as this too. You have the power to change someone's future for the better—in one sensational, supernatural moment in time.

I was dining at a Cracker Barrel a few years ago—I love that place, good food and shopping—and my two friends had already been seated because I was running a little behind. As I made my way over to the table, I passed a lady using a walker, to which an oxygen tank was hooked. I immediately thought, *She needs new lungs.*

Even though my friends were waiting for me, I stopped and talked to the lady for a minute, and she said she had COPD and lung cancer and needed a double-knee replacement. I laid my hands on her and prayed. From beginning to end, the conversation and prayer probably didn't take longer than five minutes. Afterward she thanked me and I joined my friends. Later when the lady got up and left, she was standing straight, breathing strong, and seemed to have no pain in her knees. What a wonderful God we serve!

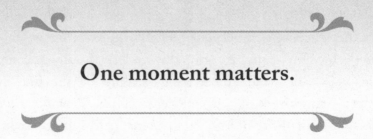

One moment matters.

A couple of days later God said to me, "If you hadn't stopped and prayed for her, that woman would have been dead in two weeks." She didn't have any idea who I was, but she knew in whose name she was healed. And that's all that matters. One moment in time.

Paul's encounter with God on the road to Damascus was dramatic. All of a sudden, boom, he was blind. Not good, right? Wow, wouldn't that be scary? But praise God, some very blessed Christians took Paul into their house, mentored him—a good word there—and told him about Jesus. He was saved and his sight returned. Paul had received a vision of what Jesus had come to this earth to do. And in that one moment in time, everything in Paul's life changed. He knew what the call of God was on his life. Everything he had been born to do was released in that one moment of time.

MORE THAN A FAIRY TALE

There once was a nice young lady who had an incredibly sweet mom and dad. But then Mom got sick and died. And it was a very sad time. Her dad did his best, but he was very lonely. He married a woman who wasn't very nice—except when she was around him. She had two daughters who were mean. After the nice young lady's father was away traveling, she was kicked out of her bedroom and had to sleep in the cold attic. She was demanded to clean the bathrooms, the fireplace, the whole house, and had to cook all the meals, although she was not allowed to eat with the family any longer. She had become an outcast.

Can you relate? Many of us can. In case you haven't guessed already, that is Cinderella's story. Jesus loved to speak in parables and God can speak through modern-day fairy tales as well. He even spoke through a donkey (see Numbers 22:28-29).

Anyway, Cinderella heard about a wonderful ball the prince was having for everyone in his kingdom. She was so excited—she knew the prince was very handsome and wanted to see him. But the wicked stepmother told Cinderella, "You're not going to the ball—we are! You are to make us three new dresses and then you will stay here and clean out the cinders from the fireplace."

No doubt you are familiar with the story, which I've put into my own words because I believe there is a godly revelation to share. Cinderella could have stomped her feet and screamed, "You can't do this to me! I'm going to the ball too!" Instead, she quietly walked out of the room and starts making the dresses.

A fairy godmother shows up. (I believe we have all had Holy Spirit fairy godmothers in our lives from time to time!) And the godmother says, "You're going to the ball and here's your dress already made." And boom, there appears the most beautiful dress she's ever seen. It even had sparkling shoes to match. Then the godmother makes a carriage out of a pumpkin and horses out of mice, and Cinderella goes to the ball. The only thing she has to keep in mind is that at midnight everything turns back to what it was, so she had to be home before the clock chimed twelve times.

At the ball, the prince saw Cinderella and fell in love with her. But shortly before midnight, Cinderella runs away. She's going so fast that she loses her shoe, which is the only thing left that the king can find of her. Cinderella had jumped in the carriage and was already out of sight. And you know the rest of the story—the prince hunts throughout the kingdom for her. And when he finally finds Cinderella, the shoe the prince has been carrying fits her perfectly. They are married and live happily ever after.

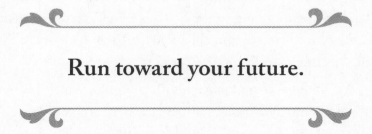

Run toward your future.

Cinderella could have gone back to get her shoe, but then the prince never would have found her. If she had gone back to her past, she would have missed her future.

How often do you go back to your past? How often have you missed God's call on your future because you were stuck in the past? When you turn to look at the past, your back is to your future. Of course, sometimes it's good to glance back and say, "Glory to God, I'm not there anymore." But don't dwell on it, don't go back and pick up your past grudges, your unforgiveness, your stress. It's time; it is now your moment in time to leave your past behind and move on into the future that God has for you.

THE WHITE DRESS

Speaking of godmothers, I have a story to tell you about a godfather.

A friend of mine wanted a white dress for her wedding. Her parents were pastoring and didn't have a lot of money, but they found a reasonably inexpensive, beautiful ivory dress and gave it to her as a gift.

"Thanks, Mom and Dad," she said graciously, but her heart was set on a white dress.

A "fairy godfather" in the church said, "I feel led to make you a white wedding dress. Would that be okay?"

"Let me pray about it, but yes," said the bride-to-be.

Wendy was married in a beautiful white wedding dress.

God uses people in your life at the exact moment when you really need something, be it a wedding dress, an encouraging word, whatever. God is always there to meet your need, just as He promises throughout His Word, the Bible. Give your worries and concerns to Him and leave them there, He cares for you.

ALL THAT REALLY MATTERS

I encourage you to step into your destiny. This is your time to get out of your comfort zone. Get out of the fog that keeps you from seeing what God has in store for you. Maybe you can't see what God has for you because you have too many things going on in your life. And maybe people keep pulling you this way and that. But take this moment in time and ask, "What does God want me to do?" Because that's really all that matters.

Does that mean you can't have a relationship with your family? No. God loves families. Or maybe you say, "How can God ever use me? I can't even keep up with my shoes." Or, "How can God use me with my horrible past?" Trust me, God will use your past in a way that will help you in your future.

God used what happened to me. And because of my past, God has used me around the world to see people set free. To see people's hearts and physical bodies healed.

My heart was healed too. Not only from broken-heart syndrome but from physical heart problems as well. I had an echocardiogram and an MRI on my heart and was told I have a perfect heart, beating 100 percent on time. At age sixty-three, I have a clean heart, the heart of Jesus.

God wants to launch you into your future, and He wants you to go out with a clean heart. He wants you to leave the junk of the past behind. Just like one of my favorite songs by Tasha Cobbs says, "Break every chain, break every chain." The first time I heard the song it was being danced to dramatically. Whenever it said, "Break every chain," the dancers threw chains on the floor. It was so incredible. At the end of the song, a man was lying on the floor as I walked toward the pulpit to speak. Afraid I would trip over him, someone started to pick him up. But God gave me a revelation just then and I said, "Leave him there, I'll be fine."

God will break every chain holding you back.

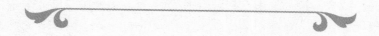

"Praise God, He set me free from the chains that held me in bondage," I said. Based on the powerful song and dance, I preached about picking up a grudge, trauma, or something that triggers our minds to go back to the past. After we're saved and set free, we can either leave the chains on the ground or pick them up and get bound up again. We have moments in time to make the right choices.

There is power in our words. The words you use today may change someone's life—for better or worse. The words you speak to yourself can either lift you up or bring you down. When you say negative things about yourself, you are prophesying negativity into your life. When you say positive, uplifting things to yourself, you begin to smile, things don't get you down so much, and you feel happy.

My book, *You Can Prophesy,* is about prophesying to yourself. What is in your head now is prophecy for tomorrow. Think about that. What you think about yourself today and God's call upon your life is prophetic to your future.

You might be saying to yourself:

- I'll never get over this.

- I'm not educated.

- I'm too educated.

- I don't have any money.

- I have too much money.

- I have kids.

- I don't have kids.

Whatever you say to yourself, remember, you're prophesying about your future. "I'll never get out of this financial mess," is prophesying your financial death. Negative, self-defeating thoughts that come into your mind are not from God or about Him. You have the choice to dwell on them or not. If you dwell on negativity, that's what you will become and what your future will become—negative, of little use to God or you.

Don't prophesy anything such as, "I'll never amount to anything." Or, "I can't finish reading these books for ordination." Come on! That's not what the Bible says. The Bible says, *"I can do everything through Christ, who gives me strength"* (Philippians 4:13).

I encourage you to start changing what and how you think. Let your mind prophesy good things about your future.

Personally, I prophesy that we will get a larger building and that more people will attend our services. I prophesy that I will mentor more people. I prophesy that finances are not a problem, but we can always use more to do what God's called us to do. I prophesy that instead of touching twelve to fifteen countries through streaming our services on the Internet, that we will touch one hundred countries at the same time.

YOUR IMAGE-MAKER

Now is the time to use your image-maker. Image-maker? What does that mean? Is that a new phone app? I'm talking about your imagination. That's your image-maker.

But God has given us an image-maker in our head so we can see our future. Personally, I see a great future for Joan Hunter. I see a great future for Joan Hunter Ministries. I see a great future for 4 Corners Conference Center. I see a great future for my children: Charity, Spice, Melody, and Abigail. I'm seeing all that, but I'm seeing even greater things. I'm seeing multiple grandchildren. I have seven, but that's not enough. I'm seeing things that Melody is believing God for. I'm seeing her living in a beautiful home with a swimming pool. I'm seeing incredible things happen.

What are you seeing in your spirit, in your image-maker? I pray that you aren't saying, "I hate my job." Or,

"Nothing ever goes right for me." Or, "I just can't get ahead." The more you say those types of words, the more they become true. The phrase "self-fulfilling prophecy" has a very deep meaning—one you should take seriously.

If you want a promotion at work, treat everybody in your department with respect, minister to them, and do your very best job. One time, someone said to me, "I gave at church on Sunday, but didn't get the promotion Monday morning. Why not?"

"Give God a couple of days," I said. "Have you ministered to all of your coworkers and served them with respect? Have you showed them the love of Jesus?"

"No."

"Well, go do that."

A month later the person said, "I ministered to everyone and I got my promotion! Now I have a whole new group of people to minister to."

See how that works? We have to expand our expectations of ourselves, not just of God. Perhaps God has told you some things, but you think, *That's a word for the person next to me. It couldn't be for me.*

There have been times when I've said, "God, did You get that right? This is Joan, J-O-A-N, not J-O-H-N. Joan, not John." I'm not questioning God on whether He got it right. It's just that I begin to think, *Can I really do all that He's called me to do?*

And praise God, with His help, yes, I can! I believe we're getting ready to go into a whole new realm in this ministry and what God has called me to do. And I'm going to take as many people with me as I can to walk into all that God has for us.

Right now, I'd like you to say these words out loud:

- "I deserve it!"

- "I deserve to be blessed financially."

- "I deserve to have peace of mind."

- "I deserve this call of God on my life, because I'm a child of the King."

God has so much more for you and for me, more than we can ever comprehend. We must forget our past and move on into our future and all that God has called us to do and to be. It's time to get out of our comfort zones. It's time to walk into what God has called us to do. It is time. Period. Why are you waiting? Why are you hesitating? He will provide exactly what you need to fulfill that call on your life.

TIME FOR PRAYER

Please read the following prayer, my prayer for you:

Father, right now, I speak over Your special and unique child who is reading this. I speak health, wholeness, restoration in every area, Father, in the name of Jesus. I speak a fireball of the Holy Spirit to fill and equip this person for everything You've called him or her to do. Father, I speak a release of revelation, a release of anointing, a release of power and direction and wisdom and discerning of spirits. I release it all, in Jesus' name. Amen.

Chapter 6

STEPS TO FULFILLING YOUR DESTINY

Thank You, Father, for today and for Your anointing on this word that You have given me to share. Father, not only anointing on this word, but a greater anointing on me and on each reader for hearts to be prepared to accept Your revelations. Father, I thank You that You honor Your Word and for Your lovingkindness and faithfulness. Amen.

I was in a service when one of the ladies began singing, "Great Is Thy Faithfulness." It was absolutely incredible and took us straight to the throne room of the King of Kings. But as I was sitting there listening, I thought, *God, great is Thy faithfulness.* And I heard right back, "Great is thy faithfulness." And I knew it was not only about God's faithfulness but ours as well.

I knew many years ago that God had called me into the ministry, more than the work I was doing in the Dallas area. God was calling me to go beyond co-pastoring a church, which I had done for eighteen years. Over and over I heard God tell me, "Get ready. I'm going to send you out."

I knew God would send me all over the world. I just knew it! So, I kept telling myself, *I have to be ready to go. God wants me to be ready for whatever He calls me to do.* I began preparing myself in the Spirit. I made sure I had a Bible all marked up exactly how I wanted it for preaching. I had my nails and hair done and even bought a new suit. I would be ready.

I became so excited that my mind went a little crazy. I saw my name in lights in Chicago, Atlanta, New York, all over. Maybe it would just be in Dallas or Carrollton, but I envisioned a whole lot more. I was so excited I could hardly stand it. I had been waiting and waiting—ready to go.

"Okay, God, I'm ready! I've done everything that You told me to do. So where are You sending me?"

"I'm sending you to the grocery store," God said.

"Well, I was kind of hoping for Chicago or New York, God, but…." With four kids, I went to the grocery store on a regular basis. "Lord, that's the last place I want to go. But in Your Word, You say that if I'm faithful in little, I'll rule over much."

God replied, "You've gone to the grocery store for all those years for yourself. Now I want you to go for Me."

Melody was still a young girl at the time, so I said, "Would you like to go to the grocery store with Mom?"

"Sure."

So, we went to the local grocery store. Going down an aisle, I said, "Melody, what do you want for dinner tonight? Melody? Melody?" I couldn't find her anywhere. Needless to say, I began to panic. Just then I heard, "Hey, Mom, come over to aisle three. This person can't hear, and we need to pray for her healing!"

I hurried over to aisle three, laid hands on the person, and prayed, "In the name of Jesus, hearing...amen." The woman thanked me, and I again asked my daughter, "Okay, Melody, what do you want for dinner tonight? Melody!" She was gone again.

"Hey, Mom! Come over to aisle seven. Someone over here uses a cane and needs you to pray for him!"

I hurried over, prayed for the person, opened my eyes, and Melody was gone again. To make a long story short, I didn't buy any groceries on that trip to the store, so we stopped for fast food on the way home. But I was faithful. As ridiculous as it seemed going to the grocery store, I did it. And then God....

No matter how small you think what God has called you to do is, you just need to do it! Be faithful in the little.

I've known my hairstylist for seventeen years. He and his wife attended our healing school while I was teaching because they couldn't have children. Praise God, their daughter, Rebecca, is now an absolutely gorgeous teenager. He uses his gift to serve others. I appreciate the fact that I can phone or just drop by the shop and he faithfully fits me in. I know I can depend on him. He allows God to use his gift—he does unto others as he does unto the Lord.

Just do it!

My motto: God will use your gift—no matter what it is.

Another example is a friend who has the gift of hospitality—and she's one of the best cooks I've ever known. Whenever I mentioned her to my parents, they used to say, "Oh, the one who cooks!"

Whatever talent God has given you, use it faithfully.

Many years ago, a fifteen-year-old came to work for my mom and dad. She was faithful to the call of the ministry. She worked all day long, and in the evening, she did her schoolwork. It took her longer to graduate than most because she only had a few hours a night for her education, but I'm sure she graduated with A's. She ran the office and the publishing company better than anybody has ever run it before or since. She was faithful over little and God blessed her over and over.

Be faithful in the little things and you will rule over much. God will give you an incredible vision of what you'll be doing. But the enemy will do whatever he can to keep you from accomplishing what you saw. He wants to abort your dream and will stop at nothing. Hebrews 10:32 (KJV) says, *"But call to remembrance the former days, in which, after ye were illuminated, ye endured a great fight of afflictions."* Or as the New Living Translation says: *"Think back on those early days when you first learned about Christ. Remember how you remained faithful even though it meant terrible suffering."*

You must be faithful—no matter what.

FAITHFUL IN LITTLE, RULE OVER MUCH

If you feel that God has revealed something that you need to do and you've had no opposition, the enemy hasn't tried to stop you—then pray harder, because it may not be of God. As Rick Renner says, "A spiritual fight usually occurs when you've been illuminated to the plan of God on your life."

Then there's a couple we know who recently uprooted their life in Washington Heights and moved to Azle, Texas. They and their staff are presently living in and running their ministry from an apartment while their house is being built. When I needed them, I called them. They came all the way to Houston to lead a praise and worship service. Even though they had a busy schedule and could have used more sleep, they came. We praised God, talked, and had a great time—and the service was full of anointing.

When we are faithful in little, we will rule over much. Hebrews 11:17 says that when God tested him, Abraham trusted God's promise and offered up his son Isaac. That reminds us that God will test us. We must be ready to pass every test.

A few years ago, I said, "God, why are You testing me? Don't You know my faith?"

"I know your faith," God said, "but do you know your level of faith?"

And through that test, I not only proved to God my faithfulness, I proved it to myself. Sometimes part of our testing is to prove our faithfulness to God and to ourselves. Are you willing, at all cost, to fulfill the call of God on your life? Don't try to escape the test by saying, "God, let this pass from me. I know You can reach right down and take me out of this." I know you may want to avoid some tests, but don't. Whether you realize it or not, the time of testing is a proving ground. Just as in school when given a test, if you pass, you move to a greater level of education. God wants us to pass each test and go on to a higher level of intimacy with Him.

It's not always easy and not everybody passes—but God is forgiving and patient.

Genesis 50:20 says, *"You intended to harm me, but God intended it all for good. He brought me to this position so I could save the lives of many people."* God gave me this interpretation of this Scripture verse: "God brought me to this position to minister to many and help them through their situation because I made it through that same situation."

I called some friends in Houston the other day and said, "I need something written in Chinese," and explained what I wanted. They faxed it over to me. The word "crisis" in Chinese is our word "together." One character means potential danger and the other means hidden opportunity. Together you have a crisis. In every situation that you go through, there's always potential danger, but there's also hidden opportunity.

I looked up "crisis" in Webster's Dictionary. It means a turning point, for better or for worse. A serious disease, which could be a physical or spiritual crisis, causes a change leading either to recovery or death. Think of a crisis not only in the natural but in the spiritual realm. Another definition for crisis is change itself. Any kind of change can be a crisis. And your crisis may be your birthplace for a miracle.

In Hebrew, the word "crisis" means birthing chair or labor, something no one can go through for you. You go through the travail of labor and birth a new life by yourself.

For example, one day during a service, I asked my friend, the hairstylist, to come up front for a moment. Then I said, "I want you to tell me what it was like, personally, to give birth to your daughter, Rebecca."

"I have no idea," he said.

"Why not?" I asked.

"Because I didn't give birth to my child."

"But you were there."

"I was a witness," he said.

"I was there, too," I replied.

"You helped deliver Rebecca," he said.

"Yes, I did," I said. "Rebecca was stuck, and I helped her out. Then I hollered for you to come in and cut the cord."

"And I cut the cord," he said.

Yes, he cuts hair and he cut the cord. And yet, his wife had a totally different experience birthing their daughter than either of us did.

My daughter, Melody, hasn't had a baby yet. Would you like her to teach you Lamaze and the best way to go through childbirth? Certainly not. You'd rather have someone like me who has had four children completely natural, to tell about my experiences. Lamaze teaches the woman how to concentrate on a focal point—or on Jesus—and breathe through the labor and birthing process with minimal pain.

I can tell you what it's like to have children. I can tell you what it's like to go through a divorce. I can tell you what it's like to be diagnosed with breast cancer. I can tell you what it's like to be codependent. I can even tell you what it's like to lose all income and financial support. And I can also tell you how God met my every need! I'd rather not have had the distressing experiences—but because I've been through them, I can tell you how God was with me every moment, and how He will get you through them too.

Whatever you're going through right now, allow God to teach you in every area so that you will learn, not only for your sake, but for those around you.

Just like Genesis 50:20 says, you'll be able to minister and save the lives of many. Yes, the devil means you harm; yes, some situations are even meant to kill you. But don't allow that to happen—rather, allow God to use it all for your benefit, your long-term good. Pray, "God, send me what I need to learn during this time because I want to get *through* it."

His Word says, *"Even when I walk through the darkest valley…."* But praise the Lord, you don't stay there, *you walk through it.* Unfortunately, too many people just stay in the valley. But not you—you will get up and go on with what God's called you to do.

THE BATTLE

During my last trip to Israel, I prayed at the Garden of Gethsemane, which is at the foot of the Mount of Olives in Jerusalem. I could feel the very presence of God there, where Jesus went and prayed in agony. When He was in that garden, Jesus knew what would happen over the next few days. He knew that a crown of thorns would slice onto His head, that He would be crucified naked on a cross in front of everyone, and a spear would pierce into His side. Do you think He had a mental struggle over the call of God on His life?

Jesus battled between His flesh and what He wanted, and the Spirit and what God wanted. Jesus ultimately said, *"Father, if it is Your will, take this cup away from Me; nevertheless, not My will, but Yours, be done"* (Luke 22:42 NKJV). Jesus submitted His will to the call of God on His life, and the Scripture continues, *"Then an angel appeared to Him from heaven, strengthening Him. And being in agony, He prayed more earnestly. Then His sweat became like great drops of blood falling down to the ground"* (Luke 22:43-44 NKJV). When we submit our will to God, an angel of the Lord will appear and strengthen us beyond words, beyond measure.

Jesus was so stressed that He began to sweat. Not just a little perspiration but drops of blood. I've been under a lot of stress, but I've never sweat blood. But I have been through the anguish of, "God, I don't want to do this. I don't want to endure that pain. I don't want...."

Yet Jesus submitted to God—He knew His purpose and destiny. He needed to go through what lay ahead of Him. And as a result, He made the way for us to get into Heaven.

Daniel 11:32 (NKJV) says, *"Those who do wickedly against the covenant he shall corrupt with flattery; but the people who know their God shall be strong, and carry out great exploits."* Don't just stay where you are. Those who know their God will be strong and can resist the devil. Take the situation you've either gone through or will go through and use it to make you stronger than ever before. And what will happen? You will do great exploits!

First Peter 4:12-13,19 says:

> *Dear friends, don't be surprised at the fiery trials you are going through, as if something strange were happening to you. Instead, **be very glad—for these trials** make you partners with Christ in his suffering, so that **you will have the wonderful joy** of seeing his glory when it is revealed to all the world. ...So if you are*

Steps to Fulfilling Your Destiny

suffering in a manner that pleases God, **keep on doing what is right,** *and* **trust your lives to the God** *who created you, for* **he will never fail you.**

My daughter Charity was diagnosed with diabetes and asthma brought on by an anti-inflammatory prescription she was given for a shoulder injury. Then she called and told me she had a serious heart problem and there was a possibility she may need a stent inserted. I prayed for her healing over the phone and then booked a flight to Nashville where she lived.

Three weeks later, I flew home when the doctors said Charity was totally healed. God proved that He can heal even through the telephone! Since it happened to be my son-in-law's birthday while I was there, we went to church, out to eat, had a birthday party, and everything was wonderful. A much better time than if we had been sitting by a hospital bed or helping with home care.

While I was on the plane, God laid it on my heart to share part of my testimony with the flight attendant. Afterward, she said, "Your story sounds like mine." Then she looked at me and said, "Did your faith in God ever waver?"

"No," I replied.

She said, "I got really mad at God once, rebelled, and walked away from Him. Have you ever walked away from God?

"No," I shook my head.

"Well, did you want to curse God?"

"No."

131

"You didn't?" she asked. "Really? I don't know how you went through all that and didn't just turn your back on God." She just couldn't imagine it not affecting me that way.

I looked into her eyes and said sincerely and gratefully, "God's the One who got me through it. What I went through made me stronger in the Lord than ever before." We talked a little longer. And the flight attendant has since rededicated her life and returned to church.

When you're willing and open, you never know where God will call you or what He'll ask you to do. Be faithful!

YOUR CHOICE

Recently someone said to me, "I think now would be a good time to drink away your troubles." She added, "But because you don't drink, that's just not an option." We laughed, but when you're in a crisis, it is easy to go to the bottle or drugs or food—or you can go to the cross. The choice is yours. Unfortunately, too many people make the wrong choice.

Outside fixes are only temporary. One day you'll come out of your stupor and reality will hit you again. So, you might as well deal with the current reality, go to the cross, and lay it at Jesus' feet. He will help you go through it and get on with your life. It's that simple.

Ephesians 6:10-17 says:

> *A final word: Be strong in the Lord and in his mighty power.* **Put on all of God's armor so that you will be able to stand firm against all**

strategies of the devil. For we are not fighting against flesh-and-blood enemies, but against evil rulers and authorities of the unseen world, against mighty powers in this dark world, and against evil spirits in the heavenly places.

*Therefore, **put on every piece of God's armor so you will be able to resist the enemy in the time of evil**. Then after the battle you will still be standing firm. Stand your ground, putting on the belt of truth and the body armor of God's righteousness. For shoes, put on the peace that comes from the Good News so that you will be fully prepared. In addition to all of these, hold up the shield of faith to stop the fiery arrows of the devil. Put on salvation as your helmet, and take the sword of the Spirit, which is the word of God.*

Put on the armor of God, the *whole* armor of God—not just the helmet of salvation to protect your mind and keep it centered on Jesus Christ. Think about soldiers serving in a war zone. What do you think would happen if all they had on was a helmet? No clothes, no guns, only a helmet. They'd be killed by the enemy.

So many times, Christians put on the helmet of salvation, but forget about the breastplate of righteousness to protect their heart. Or they have on the breastplate of righteousness but forgot the shield of faith. We need the *whole* armor of God to live a sanctified life, set apart—in the world, but not of the world.

In the world, but not of the world.

When my daughter Melody was a baby, I dressed her. But I don't dress her anymore because she's old enough to do it herself. She can decide what she wants to put on. And so can you. It is your choice whether or not you will take off the old self and put on the new self—and go out and do what God's called you to do. I took off the old self and put on the new self when I was twelve years of age. Consequently, God saved me from a life of drinking, smoking, and cussing.

A key Scripture while discussing God's armor is Revelation 16:15, *"Look, I will come as unexpectedly as a thief! Blessed are all who are watching for me, who keep their clothing ready so they will not have to walk around naked and ashamed."* We need to wear the full armor of God to make it through these end times—and we are in the end times.

We have a choice, a decision to make. What will we do with the call of God on our life?

When I was in Israel, I met a lot of Israeli Defense Force soldiers. I learned that they sleep with their boots on and with one hand on their gun. They're prepared around the clock for attack. We, too, need to be prepared at all times to go into war, no matter what the enemy tries to do to us.

Have you noticed that the armor of God described in Ephesians 6 is worn on the front of the body, leaving the back exposed? That's because we're on the offensive—we're not running from the enemy. God always sends His people to stand in the gap and He guards our back.

Matthew 11:12 says, *"And from the time John the Baptist began preaching until now, the Kingdom of Heaven has been forcefully advancing, and violent people are attacking it."* You can sit back and allow the enemy to walk all over you and treat you like dirt. Or you can get up, be forceful and take on the Kingdom of God. Go and walk out the calling of God on your life. Make that your choice. I can't make that decision for you. Neither can your spouse or your parents or friends. It's up to you.

THE TIME HAS COME

Joshua 1:1-2 says:

> *After the death of Moses the Lord's servant, the Lord spoke to Joshua son of Nun, Moses' assistant. He said, "Moses my servant is dead. Therefore, **the time has come** for you to lead these people, the Israelites, across the Jordan River into the land I am giving them."*

Can you imagine what happened when Lakewood Church heard that their pastor John Osteen had died? Many people thought that Lakewood would die, but God raised up somebody who has directed the ministry for twenty years. Joel had never preached a sermon until the Sunday before his dad died. He was quickly thrust into leadership. Lakewood Church has since grown by thousands.

In order for Lakewood to continue, John Osteen had to die. Joel used to beg his father, "Let's have a Saturday night service. Let's get more kids' programs going. Let's do...." But John said, "I'm too old to do that." Joel has added not only Saturday night services, but many other programs to reach the lost of the city.

Moses griped and murmured and complained. His disobedience precluded him from entering the Promised Land. After Moses died, God then blessed Joshua. You will see that happen again and again in the Bible. When somebody was extremely negative and wanted to stop the movement of God, God removed them. Don't let God remove you—allow Him to use you.

When Moses died, Joshua had a choice to make. He could have said, "We'll never make it into the Promised Land. Moses was the one with the dream, with the vision. Moses is supposed to take us forward. Our leader is dead." Instead, Joshua chose to rise up and fulfill the call of God on his life.

In Joshua 1:9, God told Joshua, *"This is my command—be strong and courageous! Do not be afraid or discouraged. For the Lord your God is with you wherever you go."*

Joshua made the right decision. He commanded the officers of Israel, *"Go through the camp and tell the people to get their provisions ready. In three days you will cross the Jordan River and take possession of the land the Lord your God is giving you"* (Joshua 1:10-11).

TESTING AND PREPARING

Some time ago I had to go to Dallas. I could have just jumped into my vehicle and showed up. But I didn't. I packed my clothes, makeup, vitamins, shoes, shampoo, all the stuff I needed for a week. We must take the time to prepare for what God is getting ready to do in and through us.

"Fire tests the purity of silver and gold, but the Lord tests the heart" (Proverbs 17:3), is a Scripture I remind God of often. When refining silver, it's boiled to the perfect temperature until the dross (impurities) rises to the top, which is then skimmed off. Then it's stirred and stirred until you can see your reflection in it.

I asked God the other day, "God, can't You see Your reflection in me yet? Are You sure You can't see it?"

"I'm beginning to," He said.

I breathed a sigh of relief, and said, "That's good." I want God to always see His reflection in me.

In the Book of Daniel in the Bible, we read about Shadrach, Meshach, and Abednego, the three Hebrew men the king had bound and thrown into a fiery furnace for not bowing down to him. The furnace was made hotter than ever before; in fact, so hot that it killed the guards who threw the men into it. Those three friends were in the midst of the fire and the only thing that burned was the rope that bound them. When they walked out of the furnace, they were unharmed and didn't even smell like smoke. The men came out free and unharmed because of their trust in God (see Daniel 3:19-30).

There are things that have you bound, keeping you from doing what God's called you to do. You may have prayed, "God, take me out of this. Get me out of the fire." Instead, pray that you have the strength and courage to allow what binds you to be burned off so that you have the freedom to do what He's called you to do. Be faithful in the furnace.

James 1:2-3 is an important passage—one to memorize and repeat when problems arise: *"Dear brothers and sisters, when troubles of any kind come your way, consider it an opportunity for great joy. For you know that when your faith is tested, your endurance has a chance to grow."* Be joyful when trouble comes your way because when your faith is tested, your endurance has a chance to grow.

In Genesis 41:52 Joseph says, *"God has made me fruitful in this land of my grief."* When Joseph was a teenager, he was taken to Egypt as a slave. But because Joseph was faithful to God in all that he did, God used him to save the people and his family from a devastating famine.

No matter what troubles and trials come your way, allow God to use you. And if you let Him, He will use you in a mighty way.

Someone from Florida called me who was going through a really hard time. She said, "I want you to know that God's called me to pray and intercede for you because we're going through the same thing." That brought to mind James 5:16, *"Confess your sins to each other and pray for each other so that you may be healed. The earnest prayer of a righteous person has great power and produces wonderful results."*

The caller prayed for me and I prayed for her—and God blessed both of us. We were both healed and made it through our time of trouble. And it's incredible what God has done in our lives since.

THE HOLY OF HOLIES

One night I heard a sermon about the temple, and it became personal to me. When the temple was built, it had an outer court, an inner court, and the Holy of Holies. [The menorah, filled with olive oil by man, kept the outer court lighted. But the inner court where the sacrifices were made was dark. But in order to get to the Holy of Holies the priest had to go through the darkness of the inner court and past the fine linen curtain. Exodus 28:33-35 says:

> *Make pomegranates out of blue, purple, and scarlet yarn, and attach them to the hem of the robe, with gold bells between them. The gold bells and pomegranates are to alternate all around the hem. Aaron [the high priest] will wear this robe whenever he ministers before the Lord, and the bells will tinkle as he goes in and out of the Lord's presence in the Holy Place. If he wears it, he will not die.*

When the high priests went into the Holy of Holies, the bells would make a gentle ding-a-ling and the pomegranates would make a soft swooshing sound before the Lord. The bells symbolized the gifts of the Spirit, the pomegranates the fruit of the Spirit. When we have gifts and no fruit, we're worth nothing. We need a balance of His gifts and fruit.

Something I found interesting was that a rope was tied around the high priest's ankle so that if he was not worthy to go into the Holy of Holies, God would strike him dead. Since no one else could enter the Holy of Holies, they would have to drag the priest out by the rope.

Just like the high priests, we must purify ourselves so that God can come live in our spirit, the Holy of Holies.

The temple's Holy of Holies was lit with Shekinah glory. Shekinah comes from the Hebrew word *shekinot* meaning where God settles in or dwells in, where His divine presence is. God's presence filled the temple with an intense light, a supernatural light. And when the priests saw the Shekinah glory, they began to dance around, worshiping the Lord with the bells and pomegranates creating beautiful music.

When you go from the flesh through the darkness of the valley and into the glory of God, the very presence of God, you will experience the Shekinah glory in your life. And God will light your path when you enter into the Holy of Holies.

Another Scripture to keep in mind when considering your calling is First Corinthians 15:57-58:

> *But thank God! He gives us victory over sin
> and death through our Lord Jesus Christ. So, my
> dear brothers and sisters, be strong and immov-
> able. **Always work enthusiastically for the
> Lord**, for you know that **nothing you do for the
> Lord is ever useless**.*

Also, Romans 8:37-39 confirms that God's love for us is
eternal, powerful, and victorious:

> *No, despite all these things, overwhelming
> victory is ours through Christ, who loved us.
> And I am convinced that **nothing can ever
> separate us from God's love**. Neither death
> nor life, neither angels nor demons, neither our
> fears for today nor our worries about tomor-
> row—not even the powers of hell can separate
> us from God's love. No power in the sky above
> or in the earth below—indeed, **nothing in all
> creation will ever be able to separate us from
> the love of God that is revealed in Christ Jesus
> our Lord**.*

Psalm 57:1 tells us that He will be our refuge when we
reach out to Him, *"Have mercy on me, O God, have mercy! I
look to you for protection. I will hide beneath the shadow of your
wings until the danger passes by."*

Moses told Joshua in front of all Israel, *"And the Lord, He
is the One who goes before you. He will be with you, He will not*

leave you nor forsake you; do not fear nor be dismayed" (Deuteronomy 31:8 NKJV).

God promises never to leave me or forsake me and to always support me, whether it's emotionally, physically, or financially. He will do the same for you.

God told me and I believe Him, "I'm taking you to a higher level. I'm giving you a greater understanding of the pain that you've been through and you're going to walk it out. So, line up with Me and get ready."

God will raise you up and take you to a higher level in many areas of your life—but primarily He will give you a heart of compassion to minister to our world. God said to me, "I'm preparing to reward your faithfulness beyond measure." And I saw the windows of Heaven opening up. I believe that's a word for you, too.

CONCLUDING PRAYER

Father, I praise and thank You for Your Word that has gone forth to this reader throughout this book. I speak a greater determination in this person's heart, mind, soul, and body. Whatever has kept this reader from doing what You've called him or her to do, whether it's sickness, feelings of inadequacy, low self-esteem, or even a marriage partner, I thank You right now for overcoming all these issues. I command that this reader's gifts be stirred up within and that eyes of understanding will be enlightened to all that You have.

Father, I thank You that this dear friend will walk in the supernatural and will enter the Holy of Holies where your Shekinah glory lights the way. Father, I thank You that this reader has been given the gifts and the fruit of the Spirit to walk in Your will for his or her life. I thank You for Your wisdom and guidance in this precious person's life. In Jesus' name, amen.

If you need healing, please read the following prayer out loud:

Father, You know my needs. In the name of Jesus, I speak total healing from the top of my head to the soles of my feet. I pray for the electrical, chemical, and hormonal frequencies to come into harmony and balance. Get rid of every bad cell and guide the blood flowing through me.

I speak emotional healing to my mind and heart. And I speak restoration of everything that the devil has stolen in my life—physical, emotional, spiritual, and financial. I speak a breakthrough in every area.

Father, You have provided for me and sustained me. And I curse any form of stress in my life. Your Word says that You give Your beloved sweet sleep at the right time. And I thank You for giving me greater sleep than I have ever known, greater peace than ever before.

Father, I thank You that You are renewing my mind, heart, body, spirit, and strength. Thank You for filling me so that I can fulfill the call of God upon my life.

Father, I thank You that Your Word says that you not only want me healed, but You want me whole. I speak wholeness right now, in Jesus' name.

Father, I give You all the glory. In Jesus' name. Amen.

God says, "For I have taken you through a time of stretching, of greater appreciation, and of greater learning. I have stretched you beyond what you thought possible. But your time of stress is coming to a close." Believe it!

I want to leave you with Hebrews 13:20-21:

> **Now may the God of peace**—*who brought up from the dead our Lord Jesus, the great Shepherd of the sheep, and ratified an eternal covenant with his blood*—may he **equip you with all you need for doing his will. May he produce in you, through the power of Jesus Christ, every good thing that is pleasing to him.** *All glory to him forever and ever! Amen.*

And I speak this blessing over you.

ABOUT JOAN HUNTER

Joan Hunter's genuine approach and candid delivery enables her to connect intimately with people from all walks of life. Some describe her as being like Carol Burnett with the anointing of Jesus. Her focus is to train and equip believers to take the healing power of God beyond the four walls of the church and into the four corners of the earth!

Joan ministers the gospel with manifestations of supernatural signs and wonders in healing school sessions, miracle services, conferences, and churches around the world. Being sensitive to the Holy Spirit, Joan speaks prophetically in her services, releasing personal and corporate prophetic ministry to those in attendance.

At the young age of twelve, Joan dedicated her heart to the Lord and has faithfully served Him from that day to this. She has uncompromising faith and dedication to the call of God on her life. She exhibits a sincere desire to see the body of Christ set free in body, mind, soul, spirit, and finances. Joan Hunter is a compassionate minister, dynamic teacher, accomplished author, and anointed healing evangelist.

Joan has ministered worldwide and has been a guest on numerous television and radio programs including Sid Roth's *It's Supernatural, My New Day, Everlasting Love* with Patricia King, and *Today with Marilyn* (Hickey) *and*

Sarah. Joan hosts a powerful and exciting show of her own, *Miracles Happen!*

Joan Hunter has authored more than eighteen books at the time of this writing and has recorded teachings that will encourage you and teach you how to pray for the sick and see them recover. Books and recorded messages are available to order through joanhunter.org. Some resources are available as digital downloads through Amazon.com and iTunes.

Joan and her husband, Kelley, live in the Houston, Texas, area. Together they have four daughters, four sons, three sons-in-law, and seven grandchildren. Joan is the daughter of the "Happy Hunters," Charles and Frances Hunter.

For more information about Joan Hunter Ministries, visit https://joanhunter.org/.